# Airbnb Rental Investments

*Learn How to Invest and Generate Passive Income in Airbnb Rental Home Business*

**By**

**Emily Bennett**

# Table of Content

# Introduction

Airbnb is a platform the basis of which was sharing bed and breakfast with a guest for earning purposes. This idea flourished and became the source of income for billions of people across the world. It works by providing customizable services and great hospitality. Most of the time, travelers are using this service to avoid higher expenses of hotels. It is helpful for those who are running short of money but have a plan to share their apartment. For becoming an Airbnb host, one does not need to own property and can start with a little investment or even zero investment. If it's you thinking to become an Airbnb host and earn dollars, you can start it anytime.

For earning money from Airbnb rentals, one can become a property manager by getting knowledge of digital marketing, good hospitable nature, and good business plans to share with landlords. He can also get a handsome amount of money without investment by sharing your experience with guests. If one has some talent like knowing knitting, hiking, horse riding, art, history, or even running a bike, he can entertain the guest and get bucks. Airbnb rental arbitrage is also considered a way for passive income. One can run it by building a good team, listing the accessories, increasing sales, automatization of business, or with the help of a co-host.

When someone starts working as a host on Airbnb, he must remember that hosting is not a simple job as it would require full-time availability. Firstly, he must get permission from the owner to renting and make a contract with him. He should select a place of higher profitability. If he is an owner and wants passive income, then knowing the legislation about the Airbnb in his area is necessary, as it's illegal in some countries. Making the place up to expectations of guests is the host's priority before jumping into hosting.

There are host types also. They could be opportunistic, side-hustle seekers, or even full-time re-entrepreneurs. There are a variety of roads one can go down to achieve success on Airbnb, and they all start by publishing his first list on Airbnb. First impressions put long-time effects, so presentation pictures of the place when listing must be very captivating. One can mention city name, space for the number of persons, type of house, and pricing of every accessory. It helps guests in selecting and giving reviews. Positive reviews build a good rapport, and more tenants attract. One must remember that if something has benefits, that could have some harm too. So, using Airbnb by following its rules will be a great idea.

# Chapter 1: Airbnb and How Does It Work?

## 1.1 What is Airbnb?

Airbnb is a service that allows anyone to host paying guests in a spare bedroom or a whole property for a nightly rate, just like a hotel, regardless of who owns it. Airbnb is an online platform connecting people who would like to rent out their homes with people who seek apartments in that area. Today, it encompasses more than 81,000 cities and 191 countries around the world. It comes from the abbreviation for Bed and Breakfast, or BnB, that is a fun fact for those of you wondering about the name origin. The creator wanted to recreate that in his apartment in San Francisco (a city where housing and lodgings are costly) with an inflatable mattress (Air).

There are two primary choices on Airbnb, either to get a whole apartment or to house all to yourself (of course, more expensive). But more common is renting only a room in a house and sharing it with its owners, or even with other travellers. Airbnb handles payments, IDs, calendars, listings, etc. for a minimal fee. You don't have to search people or find guests — Airbnb pays you directly — Airbnb has protections for you and your home — No experience or technical skills needed — anyone can do this. Young, old, and in retirement. Matters not. To start, it is much easier than you think i.e., you can do this in your spare time even if you work more than fifty hours a week. You can get the best reward from the lowest risk. Once I started, I had a bad loan, with almost no cash, and used other people's properties to list on Airbnb. I built a business without owning the property.

Many people get the impression that to list on Airbnb, they need their own house. But the fats are not like this saying. The company is already worth more than 30 billion, to give you an order of magnitude. The hotel business in Hilton that has been around for nearly 100 years? Twenty bn. And Airbnb has no real estate, either. The important thing you need to know is it's significant so that you can trust them. Firstly, Airbnb is not precisely the best option for all forms of travel, or at least it is not the best solution for everyone. It depends really on your priorities, and what kind of experience you like. They will try to give you some information so you can make an informed decision, and they will also clarify step by step how to use it. A lot of people prefer Airbnb because it helps you to stay like a local rather than a tourist. It gives the sense that he is a place resident, rather than just a visitor. And it's right, it's a different experience, and if the place is located in a vibrant and dynamic part of town, it can be enjoyable. It's more realistic and typically does a better job than having a hotel room to immerse yourself in the local culture. Usually, you can also use the kitchen instead of dining out at the restaurant (that can help to reduce the cost of the trip).

## 1.2 How does Airbnb Work?

- **It's a Community Based on Sharing**

Airbnb started in 2008 when three travelers looking for a place to stay were hosted by two designers who had space to share. Today millions of hosts and travelers are creating a free Airbnb account so that they can list their room anywhere in the world and book exclusive accommodations. And the hosts of Airbnb experience share their passions and interests with travelers and locals alike.

- **Services are Trustworthy**

Airbnb assists in making sharing easy, pleasant, and safe. They verify personal profiles and listings, retain an intelligent messaging system so that hosts and guests can communicate with assurance, and manage a trusted payment collection and transfer platform.

- **Provision of 24/7 Services**

In their Help Center, they answer the most common questions regarding Airbnb. And their global community support team stands in 11 different languages 24/7 to help make things right with rebooking assistance, refunds, reimbursements, their $1 million Host Guarantee, and home and experience insurance programs.

## 1.3 Why is Airbnb a Good Choice?

- **The Short-term Rental Market is Rising High**

The point towards success when it comes to real estate investments is to keep up with market trends. Recent studies show that a 7.9 percent annual growth is expected in the short-term rental market, which includes Airbnb properties, among others. Airbnb rental properties are becoming increasingly attractive for holidaymakers and travelers, as they offer several advantages over traditional hotel rentals. So answering the question, "Is Airbnb a smart investment?"- That's a good yes. As Airbnb is growing in popularity and steadily attracting tourists, renting a vacation rental property seems like the best opportunity in cities where Airbnb is not heavily regulated.

As an investor in Airbnb, you should aim to find an investment property in a prime location that guarantees a high year-round occupancy rate.

- **Higher Rental Income**

It's no surprise that Airbnb rentals have a more significant profit opportunity than conventional long-term rentals. Since Airbnb rentals are rented out overnight, the price per night is much higher than a long-term contract. Despite taking into account many factors such as the cost of vacancy and the occupancy rate, your investment in Airbnb would still make more profit. Location is the decision-maker when it comes to managing an Airbnb rental property as to how profitable your investment will be. Guests at Airbnb enjoy being close to services and attractions. Therefore, you should take into account the market you are targeting while looking for Airbnb property to rent.

- **Duality of Use**

A primary advantage of acquiring an Airbnb property is that you can use it as your residence where you can spend your holidays. It's convenient for part-time real estate investors as they can earn money from a property and can still use it whenever they want. Airbnb allows you to choose which dates are available for your rental property, something you can't do if you follow a long term rental strategy.

- **Using an Airbnb Calculator is a Best Choice When Investing on Airbnb**

If you are searching for Airbnb properties on the market, the Airbnb benefit calculator is your best friend. You can help determine the efficiency of any listed property by using the app, which is an investment property calculator. How is Airbnb, with an Airbnb benefit calculator, a good investment? The calculator measures simple metrics of real estate that can help you decide whether or not the property is worth it. The tool can predict the Airbnb occupancy rate and rental income as well as calculate the cash on cash return, cash flow, and cap rate using real estate analytics and other comparable properties. You can help grow your real estate investment business by using an Airbnb benefit calculator. Thanks to the tool's cash flow analysis, you can easily determine how quickly your real estate business will expand.

## 1.4 Ways to Get Most from Short-term Rentals

In the recent past, the short-term rental market has become competitive. Airbnb now is having more than 6 million listings worldwide, and when you're tossing out into the countless other sites— VRBO, HomeAway, TurnKey, Flipkey, and Booking.com, just to name a few— today's travelers have choices and many. As a result, for short-term rental investors, upgrading their game is becoming increasingly important, both in marketing strategy and investment approach. Want to make sure that as the competition heats up, your short-term investment estates are destined for success? Here we will discuss how you can make the most of your investments:

- **Be Smart When Investing**

Not all places are made perfect when it comes to short term leases. Indeed, if you look at current data from Airbnb data company AirDNA, it's pretty clear: finding a high-profit place to rent is more complicated than it seems. The 2018 data from the site shows a negative correlation between home prices and gross income, with households in high-demand areas such as Portland, Seattle, and Hollywood putting some of the country's slimmest profit margins. The spots with the most profits? These are in smaller cities such as Gatlinburg, Tennessee (where Airbnb's median gain is over $53 K per year), and Palm Springs, Florida (where investors will make up over $125 K per property per year). Do your proper research, and use AirDNA, AllTheRooms, and Mashvisor to narrow down on the most productive places to invest. Before investing, make sure you study local laws and housing regulations too. In recent years, some municipalities have banned or restricted short-term rentals (many HOAs also have rules against this).

Back to our central question. Does Airbnb represent a good investment?

- **Price Your Listings accurately and Adjust it Time to Time**

In the world of short-term rentals, prices are not something of a set-it-and-forget-it kind. Choosing a constant bargain-basement rate could bring travelers in, but is it going to bring profits? Likely not. Your best bet is a variable pricing strategy that takes timing, regional supply, demand, and more into account. Airbnb has a built-in tool that lets you adjust pricing automatically depending on demand, but if you seek some extra data and a more customized approach, it might be best to use an external price tool.

Here are a few of the rental devices currently out there:

o Beyond Pricing

o Price Labs

o IGMS

o AirDNA

o Wheelhouse

Make sure that your pricing is framed in a long-term context too. Sure, it sounds great to get $350 a night, but if only one out of every 100 travellers books it, then you're not making a lot of cash (and you have severe vacant positions to boot). If you're pricing it at $295 and booking up solid, you're making annual yields much better.

- **Running the Numbers**

Like any investment, numbers are the most important thing to look into before determining whether or not to pursue a deal. If you have several rental properties, just try to list one on Airbnb to see how it operates. How much does it cost you? What is the rate of occupancy? How much effort do you bring into that job? There's always the option to rent out your second home on Airbnb as well. Take a holiday, and see how hard it is to navigate the web. Just note, this stage of testing is critical.

- **Running Your Rentals Like a Business**

Whether you have one or ten properties listed on Airbnb, you should always run your rentals as if you were running a business. By what do we mean? Okay, Airbnb's are pretty much hotels, right? They are, in fact, the top competitor for a hotel. Five-star hotels are earning their reputation by moving beyond the expectations of their guests. Therefore, consider the needs of those to whom you will rent your house. An extra toothbrush in the bathroom, ground coffee beans in the coffee pot, or cold water bottles in the refrigerator are just a few ways to show your guests what you care about.

- **Be Creative**

The properties most often rented out on Airbnb are those that are well decorated and shot professionally. That way, channel your interior designer and get to work. While it's important not to become too quirky with the decor (you want to cater to the vast majority of people after all), it's perfectly okay — encouraged— to get a little creative. Is your rental situated on a "beach?" Use tiki torches and floral arrangements to play up the vibe. If you're in a town, think about hanging art that represents the character of the area.

Make sure to play to your strengths when it comes to Airbnb rentals. If you are not the best designer for the interior, outsource the job. If you are not in the best position to repair a leaky toilet, subcontract the job. Time is the most valuable asset possessed by an investor. So when you're able to delegate, you're doing what's best for you, your house, and your budget — in the long run.

- **Identify Your Target Renter**

Defining what type of person, you want your property to rent will help you market your property. If you're going to attract higher-paying guests, you will have to meet your end of the deal and provide an enjoyable experience. If, on the other side, your competitive advantage is your property's nightly pace, be prepared to work with high tenant turnover.

Whoever your ideal client looks like, make sure you play up anything about your property that you think "ideal renter" would want.

The points I discussed in this chapter are necessary for the sake of knowing about what is Airbnb. In the coming chapters, you will come across things one must know before starting Airbnb rental investments. These points will help you practice for successfully earning income from Airbnb without owning the property. So, keep your heads on what I am going to share, if you want to be a successful Airbnb host. As it's not necessary to have abundant money for starting Airbnb renting, the tips shared in coming chapters will guide you.

# Chapter 2: Things to Consider Before Investing in Airbnb Rentals

## 2.1 Location for Airbnb Investment

As with any real estate property, when choosing your ideal short-term rent, location is the most critical factor. Usually, cities with tourist attractions such as beaches, mountains, or a national park are attractive for visitors and are therefore the best places to invest in Airbnb properties. However, investors should ensure that there is less supply of hotels or other short-term rentals at the investment location. It will ensure that the occupancy rate of your investment property is high at Airbnb. Besides, it's essential to take seasonality into account before picking where you want to acquire an Airbnb investment property. You don't want to own a rented vacation home that sits vacant during the offseason and generates no rental income. In the long term, that will cost you more money than it will earn you! Successful Airbnb hosts invest in the best locations throughout the year, where tourists and other guests attend. These areas will have an apparent and high demand for rental properties in the short term.

The place is the #1 most important rule in immovable property and rental property. You can check for top neighborhoods and cities in Airbnb, but you want to know that your property is close to all the attractions you're searching for. Airbnb travelers want to get to the best facilities and to have access to public transport. If you have an ideal spot, you can also use that when pricing to your advantage. If the position is less than ideal, then render it magnificent to the house. Also, tell the travelers what they can enjoy in that area. The land may not be downtown, but it may be near a park or restaurant.

Offer as much detail as possible, and be frank about the gap between attractions. Note, this means that the prices must be very fair too.

Here are the cities considered best for Airbnb renting.

- **Cities for Airbnb Rental Investment**

Best cities to invest in Airbnb where it is legal and profitable to operate a short term rental.

- **San Antonio Airbnb**

Airbnb rentals are not restricted in San Antonio, and the town has many reasonable investment properties to sell.

- ✓ $287,760 for Airbnb Median Price
- ✓ $2,159 for Airbnb rental income
- ✓ 3 percent for Airbnb cash on cash return
- ✓ Forty-nine percent for Airbnb occupancy rate.

- **Airbnb Indianapolis**

The lack of stringent Airbnb regulations and housing affordability makes Indianapolis one of the best places to invest in short term rentals.

- Median price: $212,852
- Airbnb rental income: $1,888
- Airbnb cash on cash return: 4%
- Airbnb occupancy rate: 44%

- **Airbnb Palm Springs**

Is Airbnb perfect for Palm Springs's investment? Despite the recent legislation, the city remains a good destination for renting a rental property for the short term. Only a high median price of properties overshadows the high occupancy rate and Airbnb rental income.

- Occupancy rate: 57%
- Median price: $680,824
- Airbnb rental income: $4,342
- Airbnb cash on cash return: 4%

- **Airbnb at Fort Lauderdale**

As there is a big demand for vacation rentals in the area, short term rentals in Fort Lauderdale are a good investor. Despite the regulations, it remains profitable to invest in Airbnb at Fort Lauderdale.

- Median price: $659,772
- Airbnb rental income: $2,953
- Airbnb cash on cash return: 1%
- Occupancy rate: 51%

- **Airbnb in Key West**

Are Airbnb Investments Good in Key West? Look at the following numbers, and be the judge. If you can manage an investment property close to a million dollars, you'll receive an excess income of about $9,000 a month.

- Median price: $973,004
- Airbnb rental income: $8,710
- Airbnb cash on cash return: 7%
- Occupancy rate: 71%

If you're planning to invest in an Airbnb rental in one of these cities, surely not.

- **New York**

Airbnb regulations in New York City are relatively strict. For instance, renting properties for less than 30 days is illegal, unless the owner of the permanent occupant lives concurrently in the house.

- **San Francisco**

Implementing a policy close to that of New York, Airbnb rentals are allowed only if the owners are residents of the house. Besides, you can only rent out your home for 90 days a year.

- **Santa Monica**

After enforcing harsh Airbnb regulations, Santa Monica is best known for wiping out 80% of its Airbnb listings. The regulations require investors from Airbnb to live on the property, obtain a business license, and collect a 14 percent occupancy tax to be paid to the town.

- **Short-term Rental Laws and Regulations**

Before buying a property to rent out at any location on Airbnb, real estate investors have to check the short rent laws and regulations there. It is relevant because some cities have strict rules which make it illegal to invest in Airbnb. Only primary residents in these cities are allowed to rent out their owners-occupied properties on Airbnb and must be present during the stay. Consequently, if you are an investor planning to acquire property as an investment (not as a primary residence) and rent it out as a short-term rental, you might face legal issues.

Major U.S. cities with strict regulations on Airbnb include New York, San Francisco, and Los Angeles. On the other hand, Airbnb investors are greeted with open arms by cities across the nation. In these Airbnb-friendly cities, the laws and regulations are unlikely to affect your return on investment. It is where you'll find the perfect investment property for your Airbnb! There are four states on the U.S. housing market, explicitly authorizing and protecting short-term rentals (Florida, Arizona, Indiana, and Idaho).

You can use Mashvisor's search tools in any of those states to find lucrative Airbnb properties for sale in your city of choice.

- **Your Budget and Rental Expenses**

Possessing any rental property entails costs and expenses, which will affect your profit margin and overall return on investment. Although short-term rentals can be more lucrative than long-term rentals, they could also cost more. The most critical monthly expenses that you need to incorporate into your budget are:

- Mortgage Fees (if you choose to fund the investment property instead of purchasing it in full in cash)
- Property Taxes (these will differ by state)
- Insurance
- Furniture and Services
- Property Management Charge (if you employ a property management company instead of handling it yourself)
- Cleaning Service Fee
- Maintenance Fee
- Vacancy Provision

Indeed, the best property for you at Airbnb is the one that fits your budget. If your monthly rental income exceeds these monthly expenses, the property can produce negative cash flow (instead of a positive one) it will lead to losing money. But how can you be sure that your property really will be profitable? Quick-use a profitability calculator for Airbnb! You enter the investment costs as well as your financial details with this tool, and it will do the calculations for you. Information about the estimated rental income of the property, estimates of expenditures, cash on cash return, cash flow, cap rate, and Airbnb occupancy rate will be issued.

- **Airbnb Data and Predictive Analytics:**

One of the advantages of investing in a conventional, long-term rent is the guaranteed return that you get every month in the form of rent from tenants. Nevertheless, with short-term rentals, investors must set a nightly rate and continue to adjust it based on seasonality, special events, neighboring rivalry, and travel patterns. The fact that investors in Airbnb property don't get a fixed monthly return makes investing in those properties a concern to some.

Nonetheless, there is a way to reduce this possibility–using data from Airbnb and predictive analysis! Airbnb predictive analytics, as the name suggests, is data that helps real estate investors predict future outcomes and thereby allows them to make wise investment decisions. You can evaluate the returns and efficiency of an Airbnb investment property in the city of your choice using Airbnb analytics, based on:

o Comparable Rental Income
o Cash on Cash Return
o Cap Rate
o Estimated Rental Expenses
o Cash Flow
o Airbnb Occupancy Rates

## 2.2 Type of Airbnb Investment Property

Real estate investors know that the one that gives you the most money is the best type of property to buy for Airbnb investments. How can you define a property like this, though? It will depend mainly on the venue and the sort of Airbnb guests that you are seeking to rent out to.

For example, if you want to rent to solo travelers or couples, then a condo or apartment in the center of town is your best option.

On the other hand, if you are interested in owning an investment property in Airbnb to rent out to families or a broad group of friends, it is safer to go with holiday homes or beach houses. Perhaps worth mentioning is that you don't have to confine yourself to the conventional type of real estate. Today's travelers (especially millennials) are booking more alternative, unconventional accommodation options, according to recent studies. It includes lodges in the woods, tiny houses, motor homes, and even tree houses. If you rent out these forms of Airbnb rentals, you can give it to your guests.

- **What is the Best Type of Property for Short-term Rentals?**

In the last decade, the real estate market has changed continuously. The sudden rise of the disruptive short-term rental industry has caused a long-term ripple effect across the entire property market. Real estate investors are now more concentrated on Airbnb rentals than on the conventional rental approach, which, as a result, has sparked an increase in property prices in major cities worldwide. Extremely lucrative for investors can be renting an Airbnb apartment or an Airbnb home. But the real estate investors always seem to ask: "Which type of property is better for investment in Airbnb: An Airbnb apartment or an Airbnb house?" We have already made a discussion at how Airbnb works as a platform to understand and address the real estate query adequately. Without question, Airbnb is the most popular and trendiest type of short-term rentals worldwide. The popularity was so rapid and overwhelming that both visitors (tenants) and hosts (renters) became a significant choice. But to be successful in Airbnb investment properties, host or real estate investors must first determine which type of property is more suitable for short term rentals. Many indications point to Airbnb apartments as being the most popular and common type of Airbnb rental property. Let's see for what.

- **Airbnb Apartment Comparison with Airbnb Houses**

It is probably the main reason why real estate investors are practically choosing to invest in an Airbnb apartment property rather than a home. Generally, renting an apartment is cheaper than renting a house if we consider the same location because, in the end, the site is what affects rental property prices the most. For ensuring success for Airbnb rentals, it is typically best to purchase a property that is reasonably centrally located to attract people and make it more attractive to visitors. Giving houses on rent in central locations can be extremely expensive for guests, leading to lower cash flow over the years when we consider the return on investment, mortgage payments, or even taxes. For a guest taking an Airbnb apartment is less costly and typically produces the same rental income as an Airbnb home. The aim behind the investment is to break even to start making a profit as soon as possible. It is also a reason that the better choice is an apartment.

- **Airbnb Guests have Limits**

Until making an investment, knowing this constraint is a must for every real estate investor to produce the income he/she needs within a specified period. The investment in Airbnb is all about profit for the host, but it's also about saving the guests money, and it's the rent price that must appeal to them. Airbnb aims to make travel and hospitality a little cheaper on visitors while allowing real estate investors to make money. If a buyer buys an Airbnb house and the finances demand that he/she ask for an above-average price, this leads to a majority of potential guests finding Airbnb properties to stay at.

That is just what an Airbnb apartment does; its lower cost makes a real estate owner more versatile in adapting to the rental market and future guests' needs.

Finding the right financial balance to match your needs and appeal to your visitors can only be achieved by smart investment: An Airbnb apartment is the option here.

- **More Convenient for the Guests**

When you rent an Airbnb home, then the question that you should ask is: "What would my guests need to book the house?" There is no confined answer to this query of immovable property, but a pattern is involved. Guests book Airbnb properties based on many different factors, including size, venue, cleanliness, and feedback. The most crucial aspect of all of them is the venue, based on hundreds of reviews. If you are an investment property investor in Washington DC, then you can afford a centrally located apartment far better than buying a centrally located home. The rivalry on the real estate market is intense, and you would be forced to look into the suburbs as a real estate investor to find an affordable house to purchase. It doesn't appeal to Airbnb tourists, and your Airbnb house will most likely not even be visible given its position away from the city's main spots. The Airbnb apartment also gives visitors more flexibility in terms of a short-term stay. An apartment is typically easy to access, more secure, and central. It brings more appeal to a short rental property on Airbnb, contributing to more income for the buyer.

- **Airbnb Big House will Need More Maintenance**

It's not just a reality when it applies to an Airbnb home, but due to their bigger size, all houses generally require more upkeep and expenses than apartments. If a real estate investor is looking to make some money out of Airbnb and the hospitality industry in the short term, then placing a whole house on Airbnb can be time-consuming for the owners. Airbnb hosting includes the maintenance of a certain level of cleanliness and facilities.

It would be more difficult to own an Airbnb house because a bigger house that can have a garden or large outdoor area will be harder and longer to clean. There is also the problem of a house's repairs and maintenance, which far outweigh those of an apartment. A house would require more money to keep it always up-to-date and working. An apartment in Airbnb can be more comfortable to maintain because it is easier to clean. If you cannot wipe the apartment frequently as a host, then there are many other ways to manage it than it can be far less expensive than when owning a house. Professional property management companies can do that for the host, and they'd charge less for an apartment than a home. To tourists, an Airbnb apartment is the more comfortable choice. It ensures that visitors do not have to share living rooms or bathrooms. We expect privacy when travelers choose this choice. It's okay to provide shared outdoor facilities such as a swimming pool, garden, or barbecue area. Still, in general, Airbnb properties specified in this category are expected to offer amenities and living spaces that are exclusive to those who book a stay.

# Chapter 3: How to Earn Money on Airbnb Without Owning a House

There are many ways to earn money without owning a property. These Points will help you in letting know that what are the ways by which on Airbnb without owing any property one can earn bucks.

## 3.1 Become an Airbnb Property Manager

Property management might be a good option for you, particularly if you're a moment-rich individual. You get interested in Airbnb this way, without the hassle of investing in your own home. It's a great way to make money at Airbnb without buying any real estate. Some people want to list, but don't have the time or resources to take care of their land. That is where you'd come in. If you don't have a house or want to make your own Money On Airbnb Without Owning Land, you can become a property manager and help others who want to earn money on Airbnb by listing their Airbnb's on the web and helping them run and take a cut.

Most people want to be Airbnb hosts, but they don't have the time to handle it. Here's where a (you!) property manager steps in. Generally, your duties will include replying to guest messages, checking visitors in, updating facilities, and handing over the property after each reservation. Many property managers account for around 10 percent -20 percent of revenue. So if a one-night reservation is $150, then you'll get $30. If a one-week reservation is $1050, you're going to pocket $210, and so on. A tidy profit, but you would need 5 or 6 properties under your belt to live off this as your primary income.

It could carry in from $1,000 a week to $1,500, not too shabby. I think most people will survive on a wage like this quite comfortably. It is an incredibly risk-averse way to get started, as you don't have to have your property and focus on building your network. The significant part is that you can optimize this approach and run more than 1 Airbnb and make a big profit without losing real estate investment.

Be a Co-host with an Established Airbnb Person. A co-host is like hosting an Airbnb home, except you're more a consultant or concierge than a boss. This' title' will come in handy as being a property manager for Airbnb is challenging for some states and countries to be. The job is more of a help to an existing host. While the employee may be the same as being a full-time boss, there isn't all the paperwork coming along. It's better suited for the person who wants to get into the game every-day. The host must enter a contractual arrangement with you and assign a percentage to be sent straight to your bank account via Airbnb.

One of the best surprises as you learn to create and scale an Airbnb company is finding out that you don't need to own any property to do it. One way of doing that is to become an Airbnb property manager, also known as co-hosting.

It has all the advantages: you make money managing assets of other people, it is little-to-no spending on your part, and you can scale faster than any different model. As a manager of short-term rental properties, you are in constant communication with your landlord, employees, and visitors.

- **Airbnb Property Manager (The Regulation-resistance Model)**

Although rental arbitrage is a model of higher profit than becoming an Airbnb property manager, it is unpredictable. You never know when the rules will change and push you to turn to a rental model that is long term.

The business model Airbnb property manager hedges against this because the name is not on any contract connected to the land. In many cases, the homeowner is capable of doing whatever they like with the property — if they want to advertise it as a short-term rental, they are prevented by far fewer regulations. Plus, you have nothing to lose if laws pop up against short-term rentals. You become just another homeowner and continue to handle your property elsewhere. In your job as manager of the Airbnb house, you would only manage the property for them. You are not responsible for paying rent, insurance, housekeeping, or all that stuff that would be put upon you as a tenant or householder.

- **How Do You Become a Short-term Rental Manager?**

The first step to becoming an Airbnb property manager is to grasp the vacation rentals industry.

- **Create Your Airbnb Business Plan**

Your next move is to create a business plan for Airbnb. Plan how you'll be working with your cleaners, which Airbnb property management software you'll be using and how you'll be pricing your Airbnb listing. Can you do all of this yourself, or will you hire a team? You'll have no choice but to take on team members as you scale, if only for cleaning. You're essentially creating a company, and you're going to need a business plan to go with that. In your schedule, make sure you budget for any third-party suppliers you need to help resolve any issues your customers might have.

- **Learn Digital Marketing:**

As an Airbnb property manager, you are not only in charge of managing the property and taking care of the guests. You are responsible for the overall performance of the rental property in the short term.

Which means you'll need to practice online marketing, and probably even offline. It is not as easy as merely publishing your listing on Airbnb and then waiting for reservations. Your first step is to learn about the Airbnb SEO and the workings of the Airbnb ranking factors. You are on the right track if you can learn to write the catchiest Airbnb names, explanations, and create the most appealing picture section. You can learn how to do social media marketing after that — Instagram can work quite well for Airbnb properties. It is also an excellent point for the property to create a separate website. To do this, you don't need coding skills-you can use tools like Lodgify to create websites effortlessly.

- **A Person with Good Hospitable Nature**

Sure, people who book with Airbnb know they book with a person rather than a large corporate hotel. But that does not mean they have high expectations for hospitality. You are operating a hotel primarily, but you do not have any employees. Guests should expect things like excellent service, a spotless house, fresh towels, clean sheets, and even extra services such as a Netflix TV on it or coffee and tea at their fingertips. The whole critical thing to remember when you start working as an Airbnb property manager is that it should be your top priority to meet the guests. Ever. You can interact easily, kindly, and comprehensively and do everything you can to ensure an excellent stay for them. It will help you get better reviews, meaning more quality bookings.

## 3.2 Besides Property Manager Other Ways of Earning Money without Owning Property

- **Airbnb Arbitrage**

Airbnb Arbitrage is one of the easiest ways to invest and make money without buying a property on Airbnb.

How's it working out? It's easy to rent a landlord home, then list it on Airbnb and collect the difference.

For example, if you rent an apartment for $1000 a month, and you probably list it for $3000 a month on Airbnb, then you'll probably make $2000 a month in revenue. In this case, keeping the cost of repairs and labor, you'll probably pocket $1000.

It may not always be possible to arbitrage Airbnb as some landlords do not require subletting. You will make your relations with the landlord transparent and honest. Don't try to sneak around and try to list an Airbnb without your landlord knowing.

You'll need to spend some time finding a landlord who will encourage you to sublet.

- **House Sitting**

This one is good. As I traveled through Bath in the UK, I met a couple who are leaving every winter (I don't blame them!) and finding someone to sit and run their Airbnb at home. The listing is in its basement. The sitter at the house would live upstairs, and the listing continued to run when they were off the sun. The owners will work out a percentage based on how many bookings they have and how many three months of free rent the house sitters get to stay. It is not a bad deal.

- **Renting a Furnished House**

Airbnb Arbitrage's same technique can be used on Furnished apartments and serviced apartments. You will help them get classified and take a cut at Airbnb.

You can even partner with hotels depending on what part of the world you're in and list hotel rooms on Airbnb. Somebody I met used to making a killing to help Vietnam hotels get classified on Airbnb.

A significant advantage of listing furnished or serviced apartments is that they usually come with all the facilities you would need to get going, and your startup costs are pretty low. A rental house furnished can be your gold pot. If you want to go all nine yards and run your own Airbnb, this option may appeal to you, but you lack the funds to do so. A lot of times, a furnished rental comes with all you might need to set up an Airbnb. Extra sheets, towels, a fully stocked kitchen, and even a laundry washer. With only the basics like shampoo, coffee, and tea to be purchased out of your pocket, the startup costs will be quite low. The only challenge that you face is getting the landlord to consent to sublet their property as an Airbnb. You'll also need to look at the local laws and regulations as some towns crack down on sub-lets. But if you do your homework, there's certainly potential here without the high startup costs to make money on Airbnb. It's an interesting way of making money at Airbnb that many people are doing at the moment.

- **Helping Others Get Listed**

Go to any popular tourist spot and you'll meet a ton of people who have apartments and rooms but don't know how to market them to visitors. It is possible they haven't even heard of Airbnb. That's a vast market vacuum that you are able to fill in and make a ton of money in the process.

- **Sharing Airbnb Experiences**

Airbnb Experiences is a new thing they have promoted aggressively at Airbnb. It doesn't matter what your preferences are you can market them using Airbnb. If you're a photographer, if you like biking, you can take people on city trips, you can have an Airbnb experience as a hiking guide. The options are endless! It's a perfect win-win as they see your town from the viewpoint of a local, and you get to earn cash in the process.

- **Get Airbnb Travel Credit**

If you are going to Airbnb's invite friends section, you can earn Airbnb Travel Credit by inviting others to use Airbnb. After clicking your button, you win $20 for each person who takes a ride. What is in it for them now? Why would somebody click on your link?

Okay, they are getting $40 off their $75 dollar or more first flight. That's more than 50 percent off, sounds like a pretty darn ton to me rather than signing up at Airbnb.com and charging $75. If you have a big Instagram account or blog, the credits will add up, and you will never have to pay for Airbnb again as you collect them faster than you spend them. Although you may not receive hard cash from Airbnb, getting your accommodation always paid for is a mad lot saving you 100s of $a month.

- **Become an Airbnb Affiliate**

An affiliate program is where you get paid to refer clients to a company. Though Airbnb does have an affiliate program, they are very stringent on it and allow only those with more than 1 M monthly visits or app users, so I couldn't even get it. So guess we've got to send in the towel, eh? Okay, not.

## 3.3 Ways to Make Money with Airbnb Experiences

Airbnb has become a source of revenue for many homeowners and real estate investors. And now any Tom, Dick or Harry can get into the game and start making money with Airbnb Experiences. With no upfront costs, no development fees, and in some cases, no ongoing costs, all you need is a little experience, a creative flair and a passion for your area. Another advantage is that you can configure without having to have a marketing budget.

Simply create an Airbnb experience, and make money whenever you book. Airbnb does the rest! I know of people who have replaced their day job using the strategies that I'm about to show. If it's something that attracts you to get paid for your passions, then you have come to the right place.

Here are the ways everyone can start using Airbnb Experiences to make money. That is something anyone can do, yeah, even you!

- **A Tour to Coffee/Chocolate Shop of Your City**

Each city has a multitude of cafes, food trucks pop up, holes in the wall, and small shops selling fantastic coffee and tasty chocolate. And there's no shortage of worldwide coffee lovers and chocoholics, so you're always on a winner here. All you need to do is chart all the local hot spots that serve fabulous chocolate boutiques and coffee. Then go in and speak to the owners and hammer out an arrangement that you introduce the buyers to them, and they give free samples. Your trip is likely to be on foot, so seek to include some famous places to walk past. Point some interesting facts along the way, since there is nothing like getting info from a real local. Find out some great free resources to help you build maps like Mapme or Scribble maps. On your Airbnb Experiences account, you can share your maps with visitors and use them for making money as ads.

- **Giving a Cooking Class can be a Perfect Idea**

Hosting a cooking class with Airbnb Experiences is another excellent way to make money in your house. Even if you're not an expert or a chef, there's only a handful of recipes to perfect, and you're ready to go. Tourists simply love indulging in local cuisines.

You can go one step ahead and teach people how to prepare regional cuisine.

In this room, you will never be short of customers, which I can assure you. Stick to regional cuisines because your customers want to experience that. So if you're living in Japan, don't make a curry, you get my meaning. Have fun, and enjoy your cooking class. Consider hands-on dishes that can make your travelers messy and feel like they're part of the meal. Let them roll up rice, knead the dough, cut pasta, or fill dumplings.

- **Hiking/ Walking Experience**

If you're fortunate enough to live nearby mountain peaks, dense forests, or picturesque walking trails, then your claim to fame could be an outdoor experience. We were all in there. It could be like arriving in a beautiful city in the mountains as a tourist. You may be having no idea where to begin or what to expect. It is here that you come in! You know well the parks and all the secret paths that people would love to see. Golden goose could be something as simple as taking a group of people on a guided walk through the forest. A cold driven walk provides a possible $30 per traveler. All of a sudden, you've got an experience with Airbnb that can make you some serious bucks. If you can do multiple tours a day, or carry out large groups, then you have immense potential to make money. Why not pack a lunch or a brunch to ramp up your ride, it will draw more visitors and add to their experience?

- **Bar Hopping Tour/Nightlife**

Pub crawls are a great way to make money from familiarity with Airbnb. If you're the outgoing guy and enjoy hitting the city, it could be your wealth ticket. "Have a night out at the town and get the luxury paid for. You really can't beat that now! "For years, these kinds of tours have been around and are popular with nearly every tourist.

People enjoy visiting the best nightspots, so if nightlife is your scene, that kind of experience is for you. It's tough to find the best bars in a town you're not familiar with.

You'll often need to rely on Google reviews, or just take a chance on the street with a random bar. So here's where you get in. You build an Airbnb experience that takes tourists to all of the area's best bars and nightlife. It's a simple way to make a few extra dollars, and at the same time, have a great evening out. There is quite possible that you can even make some new friends along the way and even win some free beers from the owners. Nightlife tours are one of Airbnb's most popular activities and are one of the best ways to make money.

- **Canoe or Kayak Tour**

You may be lucky enough to live in a regional town or city which has a lake or river. You could, therefore, consider making a kayak or canoeing trip, as it is a great way to earn some extra cash. One of the disadvantages here is that the initial expenses are higher than those listed in some other ideas. For instance, kayaks can cost between $100 and $600 anywhere.

Nevertheless, for a kayak tour, the average price is about $80 per person. Hence you'd very quickly get a return on your investment. In reality, in just a few tours, you can recoup the cost of your kayak or canoe. There are lots of ideas that you can integrate into your assignments. You could do wildlife watching, eco-tours, snorkeling, landmark tours, or even just a paddle around town, for example. The options are limitless. In short, if you're nearby water, then a kayak tour is an excellent way to make money with experiences on Airbnb.

- **Share Your Passion as an Experience and Earn Bucks**

Are you a great artist? Or is it true that you can sculpt, organize flowers, fish, ride horses, or know how to make a shawl? If you enjoy art, you should make up a couple of canvases, bring some paint along and meet your aspiring customers at a picturesque location.

All you'd have to do then is give some advice (and a little champagne), and you're done. If you're an expert horseman, you could invite your travelers to come and see a working ranch and give them some horsemanship lessons. Like fishing? Take guests on tour to all the hot fishing spots. With Airbnb experiences, your passions could potentially make you a ton of money. Yeah, and the best part is you get paid to do that, which you do! It is the ultimate Job!

- **Share Hidden Secrets of Your City**

We've all been on a mill town tour that takes you to all the tourist spots you've got to duck and weave around selfie sticks. A journey that takes you to all of your city's hidden secrets where the popular tourist is enjoyably absent sounds like a lot more enjoyable. If you've lived long enough in your place, you'll know where all of the hidden gems are.

Here are some ideas that you can share with tourists:

- Old bookshops
- Antique stores
- Film
- Filming locations
- Parks Statues
- Deserted theme parks
- Graphtti walls

Get innovative with your tour and go crazy; your base of customers will want something unique and different from the same old town highlights tour.

- **Social Organizations Experience**

No, we are not talking about taking the visitors to a shelter at the nearest blood bank to feed the homeless or donate blood. Social impact programs are primarily volunteer-run and operate with groups, not for profit.

All the gains from the encounters then go directly to the organizations. Many examples of meetings with social impact include: walking rescue dogs, visiting a shelter or museum, or even writing a poem at the home of a famous writer. You wouldn't make any money from running this kind of Airbnb experience. You will, however, feel a million dollars to help the local community and charitable organizations.

- **A Shopping Tour**

A shopping tour is an easy and affordable trip to take. All you need is a little information, some analysis, and sound judgment of direction. Here are some examples of different shopping tours you may check out.

- High-End Style Outlet
- Vintage Clothing Fabric / Sewing Shops
- Premium Bargains Homewares
- The Nerd Tour (Yep, comic book shops are very cool)
- Flea Market or Farmer Market
- Antique/Treasure Hunting

- **Photography Tour**

Mobile phone cameras are becoming better and better, so nowadays anyone can be a professional photographer. Gone are the days when a big DSLR camera is needed to take amazing pictures, now you can put on a filter and go running. This technology has made photo touring extremely popular. Particularly for those addicted to Instagram. With this in mind, you might build an experience for Airbnb to draw on and make some money. So if you know your town well and have an eye for a good photo, then your next big money-maker could be a photo tour.

- **Bike Tour**

A tourist will do one of the first things when they arrive in a new place, and it's a bike tour.

You get to see the entire city, get your grips, and bookmark sites on your trip to come back to. Although running a bike tour does require a bit of capital to start with, your costs will be minimal once you've set up. On a city tour, you can charge between $60 and $150 per guest everywhere. Depending on whether you include food, and also on the length. It does not offer a bad income for a day's work, particularly if you are running multiple tours in one day. A bike tour provides some pretty good returns once you have all the logistics in place, and is one of the best-ranked experiences.

## 3.4 Ready for Making Money on Airbnb without Owning Property

And if you're looking to become an Airbnb host or start collecting some Airbnb credit, it will take you to make a lot of mistakes at the start, but you're learning from your mistakes and getting better the more you are doing it. So why not give it just a whirl and try.

- **How to Begin an Airbnb Business?**

Nearly everyone has heard of or used Airbnb— the online rental property platform that allows hosts to rent out unused, short-term private accommodation ranging from single rooms to entire houses. Airbnb launched in 2008 and has increased to include listings for more than three million properties available in more than 65,000 cities around the world.

If you have rental space open and are looking for additional income here, then how to start a profitable Airbnb business? We have discussed that how Airbnb Works? The first step, as we have already discussed, is to become an Airbnb host by uploading images and details of the rental space and registering your home.

Once a property has been classified with Airbnb, travelers who are searching for lodging in the host area can access it. Guests can explore the Airbnb listings using different criteria like:

- Location
- Dates of availability
- Cost
- Number of rooms, bedrooms, and toilets
- Amenities such as breakfast, hot tub, pets permitted, etc.
- Language of the host
- Facilities such as parking, air conditioning, etc.

Until booking a preferred accommodation via Airbnb, the guest can contact the host directly via the Airbnb messaging service for further details.

- **Internet Access**

Airbnb also has mobile applications for Apple IOS and Android devices, as well as internet access.

- **Security Provision**

Hosts have to give appropriate paperwork to Airbnb for safety purposes. Travelers can post-accommodation reviews (and hosts can look at guests) to create a supportive group. Check-ups are not anonymous.

- **Guests Services:**

Airbnb offers a secure payment channel for guest peace of mind, and payments to hosts will be postponed until 24 hours after guest arrival. Airbnb has a 24-hour hotline for guests in case any problems arise during the rental period.

- **Fees**

The host sets the accommodation price, and Airbnb pays the following costs:

- Host: 3 percent payment transaction fee
- Guest: 6-12 percent booking fee Host may need a security deposit and may also demand a cleaning fee.

- **Taxes**

Airbnb can apply federal, provincial, or city taxes on guest bookings, depending on the jurisdiction.

- **Travelers Prefer Airbnb Rentals**

One of the best things about running an Airbnb company is that, for several reasons, travelers prefer Airbnb to hotels, motels or hostels:

1. Cost: An Airbnb rental is usually considerably cheaper than a similar room in a hotel. In some cases, a whole house can be rented via Airbnb for the cost of a single hotel suite, depending on the location.

2. Live Locally: According to statistics, "live like a local" is one of the main attractions of an Airbnb stays. Many Airbnb guests prefer to stay in a community rather than rent a generic hotel room and experience the destination the way local people do.

3. Privacy: hotel guests and employees do not always surround Airbnb visitors.

4. Peace: Airbnb rentals are usually more isolated and do not suffer from disruptive hotel activity, such as early morning departures for visitors, maid service, young children, and traffic.

5. You can Take Advantage Here as You Can Visualize Everything in Advance: Unlike a hotel where you can see at best a picture of a similar room with Airbnb on their website, you get detailed photos and explanations of the actual premises.

6. Diversity: Airbnb has an enormous variety of accommodation available, from boathouses and yachts to lighthouses and chateaux.

7. The Comforts of Home: Airbnb listings have the homey feel of actual living space (some even have resident pets) rather than generic hotel rooms. Kitchens encourage guests who wish to save money on dining out to cook their food or have dietary problems.

8. Family or Friends Space: You can save a lot of money with Airbnb by renting a whole house/apartment/condo for family and friends, rather than several hotel rooms.

- **Is Renting Permissible in Your Area?**

You must be sure that it is legally allowed to become an Airbnb host in your jurisdiction before you decide to start an Airbnb company, and you are prepared to follow local laws and regulations! Local laws on hosting paying guests can vary greatly depending on your city/state or provincial rules— in some places, and they have banned altogether. In contrast, in others, they are subject to an occupancy tax. If your room is an apartment or condominium, be sure to see if you are allowed to sublet the premises. Landlords of condos and condominium societies often have rules in place to prohibit owners from renting out their units as spaces for Airbnb. Renting your apartment can get you evicted without the approval of your landlord. Neighborhood partnerships are also a significant concern. A few disruptive or thoughtless Airbnb guests can quickly turn you into a neighborhood pariah. If none of these problems are insurmountable, an outstanding home-based business opportunity can be to become an Airbnb host.

# Chapter 4: Airbnb Rental Arbitrage

In the previous chapter' we have discussed how one can start earning passively on Airbnb without having property. It was briefly described that how a property manager on Airbnb can be a big benefit. I also told you about getting bucks by sharing your experiences with guests. Yes, that is a fun way to entertain others, along with enjoying your talent. In this chapter, I will share another important way of earning, and it is Airbnb rental arbitrage. Google searches for the word "what is rental arbitrage" are over a million.

For a good reason: You can start with some fair savings with an open business model with high-profit potential. You can maximize the short-term rental market without owning property.

There are three ways to do this:

- Property management
- Sharing your experience
- Rental arbitrage

We have already discussed about the first two points. Now, we're going to talk about how Airbnb arbitrage may make money. In short, corporate rental arbitrage is the practice of renting a long-term residential property and then renting it again on Airbnb or other short-term rental sites as a short-term or holiday rental.

Making money on short-term rentals is not exclusive to those who have been born rich or who have assets already. That's why I am talking only one approach today to scale your Airbnb company without property ownership. It is one lovely explanation that more and more people will list on Airbnb: rental arbitrage. And anyone can get in on that.

## 4.1 What is Rental Arbitrage and Profit Potential?

It is straightforward math. When you pay less in monthly rent than what you would rent your apartment on Airbnb (which is often the case), you have good rental arbitrage business potential. For example, you are currently paying $2,000 a month for your San Diego one-bedroom. On Airbnb, the prices are around $170/day for the same type of apartment in the same location. With just 11 days to do this, you will pay your entire deposit! You could make a profit of $3,000/month if you move in with your girlfriend and rent out your apartment fulltime. It is a rental arbitrage.

- **Benefits of Rental Arbitrage**

In today's economy, fewer and fewer people can buy homes. The costs of purchasing a home are not only rising across the US, but the median wages do not reach the amount necessary to be able to purchase homes. The average salary needed to purchase a home is $61,453.51, but the average US wage is $47,060. It prohibits many people not only from owning a home to stay in but also from wanting to take the conventional short-term rental path (which could potentially buy a home with its profits!). Thankfully this is not the only way to purchase land.

Now, even if you can't afford to buy a house, a property can be rented from a landlord, listed on Airbnb, and pocketed the difference. It is estimated that Airbnb has more than 150 million users and was last valued at $31 billion. That is a lot of potential for the company. For everyone except hotel owners, this is a win-win. Users need a short period to live somewhere, and hotels are too costly. However, with business as well as leisure travel growing, people want to stay somewhere where they can feel at home. Why not rent your rental apartment?

- **Profit Potential**

Airbnb arbitrage has a strong potential for profit.

If you are doing your homework, pick the right properties, find enthusiastic landlords, and handle them well, you can expect to make around 1.5x − 3x your rental cost. So if you're renting a $2,000 apartment, spending $5,000 (minus $1,000 in expenses), only one property will make $2,000/month. You could make $20,000 a month at ten houses because you've found the right landlords in the right areas.

- **More Autonomy**

In addition to the higher profit potential, the advantage is that, unlike the business model of property management, you will not have to rely on your clients— the homeowners whose Airbnb businesses you operate. For example, as a property manager, if you have ten properties and suddenly 5 of your customers want to go with someone else, you are going to get hit hard. With that in mind, you have to keep your customers happy − on the weekend, and they can suddenly decide to let their mom use the room, even though you've already rented it out. There's nothing you can do on that. You're completely independent with the leasing arbitrage. Just have to have the landlord pay rent. And you're making the break 100 percent.

- **Get Knowledge That is Rental Arbitrage Legal?**

In many cases, Airbnb arbitration is perfectly legal. But not all of it. And sometimes only in specific circumstances. You can review the laws on the Airbnb website itself, where you can also find contact details for local authorities.

You can also get details from Google about the regulations in the property town you'd like to rent. There is no administrative workaround or database. They are all different; each jurisdiction has its regulatory framework. You have to do the job.

You can do the above or go to the town hall and ask directly what the rules are. Real estate arbitrage was a technique employed by many in the long term. The critical point is to ask the landlord to ensure that they are on the same page as you. Some will be, some will not be. Ask before you rent, and move on to the next property if they do not like the idea. I have had several questions when I first come across this pattern. I worried if it was lawful or how, when they find out, the landlord will react. When looking back, the questions seem ridiculous. But whosoever wants to break into this company must tackle them.

So, the answer is yes to the first questions! It is legitimate.

In reality, arbitration of immovable property is a technique that has long been used. Very often, it is just not spoken about. It comes from the field of commercial real estate, as do many innovative investment strategies. The only thing you need to do with the landlord simply tell them what your intentions are with the house. Some are open to it; others aren't going to. When you come across someone who isn't, you step on. The aim here is to approach it honestly.

Now that we know the business model is legal and ethical let's immerse ourselves in the details.

## 4.2 Business Plan for Rental Arbitrage

The most difficult and foremost task is to search out properties that:

1. Are at a rentable place

2. Have a buy-in with the landlord

3. You can use apps like Mashvisor or Airdna to determine the best areas for properties, and then you have to do the dirty work yourself to go out to the landlords to negotiate what you're going to do with their rent.

You can then start listing your property on Airbnb and other sites, use software to automate most of the activities, increase sales, and optimize your Airbnb for greater visibility.

When people typically consider investing in real estate, they usually assume a couple of things.

1.  They think they need a lot of capital to get going,

2.  To make money, they think they need to own a lot of land. Although owning a property and having a lot of startup capital is certainly not a bad thing, the model I'm about to give you is really important, and here owning property is not essential.

- **What is Airbnb Rental Arbitrage?**

Let me present a groundbreaking investment strategy known as Arbitrage Airbnb. The word arbitrage is a financial concept that essentially means taking goods from one marketplace and selling them into another for a profit. It is when an individual leases property from a landlord, then lists it on Airbnb and receives the difference about Airbnb. For example, if you rent a condo for $1,500 a month, then list it for $4,500 a month on Airbnb, then you earn $3,000 a month before expenses. Based on your plan, the costs will vary from $250 a month to $1,000 or more. Many rental arbitrage investors aim to make a net profit of about $1,000 per property— though you can make a lot more.

- **Business Facts of Airbnb Arbitrage**

Firstly, I would give you some statistics regarding the entire Airbnb market. A lot of people think that the industry is just a fad or short-term disruption. Most people talked about the internet, smartphones, and even motor vehicles the same.

I'd like to convince you this business doesn't go away anytime soon. In reality, the business of home-sharing and short-term holiday rentals is booming like never before.

If you don't already remember, Airbnb is an online community and marketplace that allows people around the world to list and book short term accommodations. It was founded by Brian Chesky, Joe Gebbia, and Nathan Blecharczyk in 2008.

Airbnb is estimated to have more than 150 million users as of 2019 and was last valued at $31 billion. There are listings of more than five million properties in 191 countries around the world. That's more than the five most prominent hotel brands combined, by the way! And, as you can see, Airbnb has been a significant disruption to the market in the short term and is now transforming the entire industry in a way that can make you very rich in the process.

For starters, let's take a look at the story of Pol McCann, a Sydney, Australia 52-year-old host who first used Airbnb as a guest while on a trip to New York City. For a fraction of what he'd spend on a hotel, he was able to rent a studio apartment in Manhattan. He loved his trip so much that he wanted to list his residence after returning to Sydney. He cleaned it up a little bit, took some pictures, and had his first reservation within 24 hours. A single flat will remain booked for an average of 28 days per month. After six months, the money he made from his first listing allowed him to buy a second apartment across the street at the same building. Today McCann reports that after expenses, he receives about $100,000 a year. A six-figure business is a relatively good first-year profit!

## 4.3 How to Get Start in Airbnb Rental Arbitrage?

I stated in the beginning that you need not be a homeowner or have access to a lot of capital to get started with Airbnb. That is because the costs of selling the first property are relatively low. Besides, we will be using the properties of other men.

Now I am sharing essential points for staring rental arbitrage:

1. Start The Business

2. Build a Team

3. Marketing research

4. Properties to Find

5. List Resources

6. Sales Benefit & Optimization

7. Automatization of your business

**1. Setting Up for Business**

One thing you want to grasp first is that this is a legal affair. Some people have the misconception that building a rental property portfolio on Airbnb is not a "true" business anyhow. That's not at all true, especially if you want to do this professionally. If you want to set your portfolio to more than three assets, then you should properly start your business. It means providing the right foundation and infrastructure to function in good standing and to develop effectively.

The first thing that you can do is create a legal entity. I find that the LLC works best for most people, because it's easy to set up, easy to manage, and has favorable tax choices.

Establishing an actual business will help you get more offers later when you start looking for a property. Many property management companies won't let you conduct this business model without a corporate contract. If you would do this, though, then you'll have access to opportunities that amateurs won't.

You'll require to take inventory of your properties, tools, and network at this stage of the process that you can potentially use to help you succeed when you start.

You're ahead of the curve if you already have a second property you don't live in. Depending on their location, rating, and zoning, you may be able to turn this property into your first listing. However, to get going, it is not essential to have an existing property. You don't need a lot of dollars to get started in that market, as I said before. If you have quite a bit of investment capital already, then I encourage you to start small. While it is tempting to leap first into the business head and throw your money at something, you must first know the structures before you scale. All that's required to get going is about $1,000 to $2,000 in capital-wise terms.

## 2. Building a Team

You'll need a good team, like any good business owner or real estate investor. When you're just managing one house, it's easy to handle it yourself in the beginning, but once you start to scale, you'll need to rely on your team. Your core business staff should be your accountant and your attorney. You will look for someone who specializes in corporate and real estate law when seeking an attorney. If they have prior experience with real estate developers and other rental property owners, it is even better. The same goes for your accountant as they should understand tax strategy and have real estate investor experience. Such two members of your network will help guide you through common pitfalls that many beginners find themselves in.

It is time to start expanding your team until you scale out to three or more properties. Here are a few of the prominent members you'll need:

- **Co-host**

A co-host is an Airbnb user who does not run any property by himself but allows full-time hosts to handle their existing properties.

The co-host is your property manager, who is assisting you with the day-to-day business operations. Airbnb allows you to send a portion of each deal's income to the co-host with which they support. If you have many properties throughout the city or in different markets, you'll have several co-hosts who handle their little piece of the pie.

- **Cleaning Team**

You can clean your property in the beginning; however, this is very time consuming and will not be practical once you have more than three properties. When it comes to finding a cleaning crew, you have a few choices. You can find a professional company to handle the job, or you can find an employee or small business. Both have their benefits and harms, so you have to decide what makes sense for you and your company. Mom-and-pop cleaning crews are usually more adaptable and cheaper, whereas specialist companies pay more but are more efficient and are more accountable.

- **Other Members**
  - Landlords and property owners
  - Real Estate agent
  - Bookkeeper
  - Interior designer
  - Contractor
  - Photographer

## 3. Marketing Research

For days, I can talk about market research, as it is one of the most critical steps in this whole process. Many people who enter Airbnb do not do any market research beyond a Google search— if that is the case.

Only because you have a suitable property and think it's in a great part of the city doesn't mean it's going to be successful. To locate property in the most desirable parts of town, you need to use hard facts.

You choose to check out which submarkets, zip codes, and streets to give you your buck the most significant bang! If you've been going to skip any steps and hurry through the process, I'm telling you: don't skip off solid research in the business. There are many ways to find the details you want when determining where to purchase a property. Some of these approaches are free; others can be very costly. By raising your investments and increasing your cash flow, you'll be able to invest in more advanced market research methods. Nonetheless, you may be a little more constrained about what you can afford when you are just getting started.

- **You can take help from Airbnb Website**

The Airbnb website will give you a lot of details about your region. You've just got to know what to look for. When you open the site and look for homes in your area, you'll see a map with different filter choices. You'll have to choose "Entire Home" and create a property filter with a minimum nightly rate of $100. It is because we are not starting a room-sharing company. If it is your business model, then you can go ahead with it, but we're generally talking about renting the whole building. With this approach, you'll be making more money. As with the minimum nightly rate of $100, this is what you want to use to search out where are the most in-demand properties. I want to estimate a 50 percent worst-case scenario occupancy and still be competitive, and typically a nightly rate of less than $100 does not cut.

Now you're going to want to look for listing clusters and go one by one through them to create a pattern. Many markets may require specific types of property, number of bedrooms, facilities, proximity, style of decoration, etc. During your research, your job is to find out those stats and then model those statistics in your business strategy.

Discover the things that people in your town talk about, possibly beaches, parks, restaurants, or bars. This information can be found in the explanations of the top Airbnb listings, the ratings, and with Google searches on different travel pages. It provides you a better idea of where you want to start looking for assets.

First, you want to measure the possible profitability of your application listing and demand checking. If you can still be profitable at a monthly occupancy of 50 percent, then your property will likely be useful. If the nightly rate at your target location is $200, then you'll get $3,000 for the month for 15 days of bookings. If your rent and taxes are $2,000, then for the month, you'll be netting $1,000. For a 50 percent occupancy, that's pretty good and doesn't even account for the additional costs that you'll charge the guest (like a cleaning fee). Find out what the rents will be for your region, and run your numbers. There are tools for checking occupancy and demand, but with the Airbnb app, you can still do it for free. When you look at multiple listings in your area and look at their potential bookings in the future for one or two months, you can get a decent idea of how they do it. To do this, just right-click the "Check-in" button near the calendar. Instead, the navigation arrow loops through the months. The days you book will be filled in, and bold text will be the open days. There's a lot more going into market research, but that's enough to get started.

### 4. Finding Properties

Now that you've gathered real market data that shows you exactly what places are most competitive, what types of homes people want, what attractions people want to be close to, and so on, it's time to find your first house. At first, locating a property can be like looking for a needle in a haystack, but the market data you have gathered earlier can help with the search down.

## 5.  Listing Your Home and Its Accessories

It's relatively straightforward to list your house. Just follow the instructions on the Airbnb website by choosing "Become a Host." To get started, you can create a dummy profile and then create your original listing. You will build your schedule, guest specifications, and regular prices once you're set up. Once you have set-up, the Airbnb website and app takes pretty much care of everything.

Having done all the company backend activities is what makes this model so quick to get inside. You can start optimizing your listing from this point so that you can draw more visitors to your house.

## 6.  Increasing Sales and Airbnb Web Optimization

Now that you've put up your property on the Airbnb platform, you can start to customize your profile to attract more visitors. That profile has a rank that is calculated by an Airbnb-only known internal formula (just like the Google search results). Inside the algorithm, there are many known white hat methods to increase the rank and attract more guests. Having great pictures is one of the most important things you can do to increase the number of people who click on your page. If, for a couple of hundred bucks, you can hire a professional photographer, then do it. If not, then consider borrowing an expensive camera and learning a bit about lighting and editing photos. The pictures are one of the first things that people note when they click on your page. So they can be a decisive factor in whether visitors book with you or not. If you want good examples of high images and top-of-the-line listings, then click the "Airbnb Plus" homes to show your market's top-rated properties.

To have a good idea of what your property will look like, search through the properties at Airbnb Plus to see what's successful. Should people use specific keywords in their titles? Will they view the living room, bedroom, kitchen, patio, etc.? Is there a trend in the interior design that stands high out in the market? You can ask such questions from yourself, and do your best after the top performers to model your profile. A lot of people that enter into Airbnb, they wing it and try to come up with everything on their own. For this reason, most people are getting mediocre results. When you put a little time and effort into successful market research, marketing, and interior design on the front end, you're going to be doing very well.

## 7. Automatization of Business

It's pretty awesome to effectively build a portfolio of multiple rental properties that produce thousands of dollars a month, but being stuck working 100 hours a week to maintain it sure isn't. We didn't get into business and spend so we could do two or three times as much work as anybody else. We did it because we wanted life to have independence, autonomy, and choices. Putting in place the right systems will allow you to run your Airbnb business with minimal effort and keep making a reliable income. Luckily, Airbnb manages a lot of the technological aspects of the booking process for you, but there is much more that you can do to remove yourself from the daily operations.

Automating your company is all about the processes and systems you and your team develop. It also comes down to some essential tools and applications for streamlining the process.

Once you've set up your property, it's just a matter of keeping the necessary property management tasks and a continuous cleaning process after each booking.

If your landlord has a property manager or you are using a condo in a building, then it will take care of your basic property management needs. If not, then you need to find a suitable property manager who will be able to handle these issues. The cleaning crew needs to understand whatever needs to be done every time they show up for cleaning. It would help if you also learned when to show themselves and get the job done. The better method to do this is to synchronize your Google calendar with your Airbnb schedule, then swap your cleaning crew with a "read-only" version.

We can view the calendar this way, but we can't change it. It will give them what they need to show up on time after each booking without you need to prepare. However, as you shared it with them, if you have to find a different cleaning crew later, you can also revoke access. Your next most important strategy of automation is to get a co-host. In the team segment, I briefly mentioned co-hosts and how they can help you run your business. You want to find someone you can trust, who has expertise in the hospitality and property industries as well. That person will be your business face on the assets they serve and operate. They will be responsible for handling questions concerning visitors and providing additional services. They are an internal provider of Airbnb properties for you and your listings.

If you have several listings in multiple markets, then you'll have more than one co-host running your portfolio site. You are increasing employ a CEO or asset manager after a particular stage, who will handle your job of looking after and growing the business.

First, you want to have the check-in process automated. The last task you can do is driving to your listing personally. Then you have to welcome every single guest who stays at one of your properties.

The way you get around that is by allowing your guests to have a self-check-in process. To do this, they'll need access to the keys to enter the property upon arrival. You can either use the old school lockbox used by real estate agents or use smart locks. The lockbox downside is people can lose the key or come back months later to rob you. The upside of it is they're cheaper. You would have many choices when it comes to smart locks and a lot more security features. The August Smart Lock is a popular model, costing you a few hundred dollars. For smart locks, the property can be accessed remotely from your phone.

You can give temporary codes that expire after your visitor leaves, and you can see who is using customized systems to enter the property too. It gives you much more transparency and control when handling your land. Another secret to automating your company has a detailed manual for your home. The manual on the house is something your visitors will have access to once they book with you. A successful house manual will answer any issue that a guest might have so they don't feel the need to email you. It should have everything from Wi-Fi passwords, gate codes, and facilities accessible to local attractions, transportation options, emergency contacts, contact information for the co-host, etc. The handbook offers your guests all they need to be self-sufficient. When they're staying at your house, most people don't want to be bothered, just as they wouldn't be in a hotel. Make it easy for them to get what they need by providing them with a detailed house manual without too much effort.

# Chapter 5: Hosting on Airbnb

Hosting is luckily an excellent on-the-job or training opportunity for those with no experience in the hospitality sector. Hosting teaches skills in business, marketing, communication, property management, and customer service, from planning your room to designing your listing summary to interacting with visitors. You'll also hear about your principles, expectations, and goals and how to keep the pressure on your control. As satisfying as it's been to learn as I go, I would certainly have saved my time, money, and energy if I knew a few key things before I jumped in blindly. Not to mention, Airbnb isn't suitable for everyone or any room, so you'll want to proceed with caution, particularly if you're unsure if home-sharing is the best option for you. I created a list of things to help you make an informed decision, which would have helped me when I was just getting started.

## 5.1 Things to Know Before Becoming Airbnb Host?

- **Hosting is a Hard Work**

Hosting is a physically, mentally, and sometimes emotionally draining job that requires tremendous concentration, time, and energy. Be prepared to respond promptly to guest inquiries (you need a reliable smartphone and adequate data; Smartbnb will help!) and to deal with problems immediately when they occur. You— or a trusted property manager— must be available 24/7, and at the notice of a moment.

- **Goals and Intended Outcomes**

Find your revenue and occupancy goals for the month.

• How much money are you looking for / need to make?

• How often are you going to have to rent out your room to achieve the objective?

- Is your market occupancy target practical, and your turnover management capability? AirDNA may be used for market data.

Consider the experiences you want to have with your visitors– and which are that you want to avoid.

- **Hosting Like Running a Small Business**

Home-sharing includes marketing skills, customer relationships, communication, property management, and 24/7 availability. You are going to have to learn what you don't already know. It may be necessary to hire professional support.

- **Knowing Airbnb Policies, Procedures, and Guidelines is a Must**

Carefully peruse the software, to make sure the system and environment are working for you.

A whole segment is dedicated to:

- Hosting
- Trust and Security

- **People Judge You by Your Presentation, So Proceed with Great Caution**

Even if you're planning to share space in your private residence or not, hosting requires excellent communication skills and the ability to communicate with people in all sorts of situations. Reserved and people from us with a low social contact threshold need to set limits for visitors and be realistic about what we can cope with.

- **Unforeseen Circumstances, Disasters, and Do-overs are Unavoidable**

Be ready to navigate the hiccups gracefully and have an emergency supply plan.

Most of all, you're going to develop tools to deal with stress without losing confidence in front of guests. It would help if you did it to avoid regretting yourself up for errors before guests. Even the most seasoned hosts are unable to predict clogged toilets, power outages, or fallen trees. Along with doing your best to have a disaster management plan, you'll have to understand that there are certain things you can't account for.

- **You Should have an Emergency Support System for Plumbing, Electrical, and Other Issues**

Get reliable references, and make a relationship with these folks before listing your room. Make sure that this dream team gets paid handsomely and well. If they are trustworthy and provide quality service, they are worth their weight in gold!

- **You would Need to Maintain a High Quality of Cleanliness**

Be prepared to preserve the room as if the professionals are cleaning it up. It involves the spotless keeping of bed linen, mats, pillows, and secret areas. You will also need to consider the cleanliness and overall appearance of any space that visitors can see or navigate – indoors and outdoors. Isn't it a shame that a guest gets upset because the toilet has been ignored or neglected? So be careful when it comes to washing. Clean every nook and cranny, and twice clean the bathrooms. You don't want to lose income or positive reviews just because they didn't clean the property correctly. Please hire cleaning services such as MaidThis! To ensure the transition is done in a useful and timely manner. The company takes care of places where visitors pay the most attention and how to meet their needs. Even when you are low on supplies, Airbnb will let you know.

- **It Takes Time to Develop a Routine and Learning the Ropes**

You might not necessarily achieve all of your goals and expectations. Practicing patience and turning to support from Airbnb will keep you calm and empowered while you construct your unique business model.

- **You may Encounter People who do not Evaluate Your Time and Effort.**

Could you not take it for yourself? It could be particularly challenging if visitors share space where you stay, or you tend to feel sensitive. Luckily, you don't have to sell your space to anyone who is rubbing you the wrong way. Know how to detect guests having a problem based on their profile.

- **Guests are the Customers and are Not Your Friends**

No matter how warm the report is, or how bonded you feel, you have to view it as paying clients. Training to provide friendly, professional, and personal service is a beautiful hosting feature that enriches your lives.

- **You have got More Liability**

As an investor in real estate, your responsibility does exist, but it is based on tenants and your physical property. You are getting increased risk for Airbnb. People may take the items your unit has been furnished with. Can the neighbors complain? Various laws and regulations are to be considered. You could run the risk of squatters. And a whole lot more. For everything, there is a risk, and the secret to mitigating risk is you got it, information. You must know your duty and take steps to minimize it.

- **If You Are Relying on Airbnb Income, planning for Slow Seasons is Necessary**

Whether you are carefully budgeting, raising your prices, or bringing in a long-term visitor, creating a plan to get through unavoidable slow periods is key to maintaining desired sales.

- **Setting Boundaries is Crucial to Success, Sanity and Security**

It is a great idea to get clear on your physical and emotional boundaries before listing your place. If you have difficulty setting limits, you'll need to learn how to do so effectively. Luckily hosting offers endless possibilities to know!

## 5.2 Common Characteristics of Most Successful Rentals on Airbnb

By contrast, Airbnb remains a relatively young business concept, with its origins rising deeper into the sharing economy every year. The youthfulness of the short-term vacation rental means that there are still no strict and hard rules that renters and hosts have to abide by, meaning that the rental situation of one person can look drastically different from that of another. With such a wide array of Airbnb options out there, let's look at some of the specific attributes that set apart from the rest of the most popular Airbnb's.

- **Size of Accommodation Matters**

It's a fairly obvious idea that a host that provides just one room on Airbnb can produce substantially less revenue than a host that offers a whole house or apartment. But have you known a multi-room rental would generate almost 100 times more income than a single room? It also seems that there is a significant increase in popularity for hosts with multiple listings available, compared to having only one listing.

Almost one-half of all Airbnb bookings are going to hosts with various listed properties (i.e., as a "private user" or "skilled host"). In the simplest terms, more is created by those who give more (as in more than one room or a posted listing).

- **Location, Location and Location**

Since not every city can demand Airbnb prominence like others, and while it's unlikely you're reading this and dreaming about rooting out of your home to meet the needs of the world's most famous cities, there are a few standard features of some Airbnb world "hotspots." Miami and San Diego were recently ranked as America's top two most active Airbnb cities. Both coastal towns enjoy warm weather and relatively affordable housing, and this seems to be a winning combination in the rental industry for short term holidays.

- **Rentals that Look Good Give Good**

Hosts investing time and money in professional images of their rental properties produce considerably more revenue than properties providing no pictures or showing only amateur snapshots of their available spaces. Time after time, with the addition of well-shot, skilled images, the landlords and rental agencies have seen an immediate increase in traffic and interest in rental properties. So take the time to research a local short-term rental photographer, spend the money, and be confident that your investment will pay off big in the long run.

- **Focus on Sharing the Experience**

Change your attitude a little. Change the perspective from "I'm just renting out my room/basement/house" to "I'm selling an experience." Remember, visitors are not only interested in seeing the famous churches or museums that your town is known for, but also have a genuinely "local" experience. Please consider planning something similar to a guesthouse guide that highlights some of your favorites.

There are many investors in real estate rentals, but not all of them are businessmen.

Renters are the ones who have transformed short-term rental opportunities into a full-blown enterprise, creating a repeatable and reliable method of sourcing and running a whole portfolio of profitable short-term rentals on sites like Airbnb.

- **They have Multi-Unit Goal**

The successful entrepreneur NEVER compromises for just one rental unit in the short term. They may start with one to learn and refine their craft, but the goal is to keep adding units until they hit a portfolio that spits out cash flow like a broken slot machine. Are you a casual renter just looking to make an extra buck? Or are you trying to build your rental empire over the short term?

- **They are Putting Full-time Effort**

While the re-entrepreneur may begin part-time, the aim and objective are to make a full-time effort on short-term rentals before they reach their target portfolio size. Bids on a part-time basis will yield partial benefits for you. You cannot create a viable portfolio of short-term rentals in multiple units without putting some significant time and effort in front.

- **They Build Systems to Automate**

From the very start, successful entrepreneurs are looking for ways to expand into their short-term rental business in automation. Their time is very important, so they're willing to give up some of their unit income to free up time for more units to be found.

The "Four Hour Hosts" prefer to use SmartBNB for their automation needs–this is a Ferrari for the price of a Corolla in the world of Airbnb automation.

- **Employs Leverage**

The businessmen do not seek to do everything on their own. They are trying to find someone who can do it more quickly and cost-effectively than they could alone. It means they are going to try and find the best suppliers to outsource laundry, maid services, and even check-in / check-out services. Does that mean they're paying for services from third parties and having to cut to their margins? Hey. But it does mean they have more time to find another unit.

- **They Optimize Profit per Hour**

They concentrate on maximizing their income per hour, and NOT their profit per unit. Why? To what? Since optimizing the server income requires even fewer overall units than can be handled by themselves. It's about maximizing the whole money we can make in their company to the most effort they can put in.

- **They are Entrepreneurs**

In a well-defined space, the essence of all effective entrepreneurs is that they are only entrepreneurs with a well-defined objective. They are resourceful, imaginative, and have a lot of hustle, most of all.

## 5.3 What are the Financial Expectations When Becoming a Host?

There are several further issues to consider before making a final decision to host on Airbnb:

**1.** Do you want a business to start? Starting an Airbnb company is like starting any business— you need passion, entrepreneurial spirit, and willingness to put in the required effort, starting with doing the necessary background research and making a business plan.

**2.** Have you got the time? Being a landlord can take a lot of time, particularly for short-term leases.

You need to:

- Manage your bookings and reply to potential renter communications
- Have guests meet to give out or collect keys
- Make sure the property is cleaned properly and ready for guest arrival, including fresh linens, breakfast supplies (if applicable). Manage all property maintenance issues such as plumbing and pest control, electrical repairs, and repairs to appliances
- Be available on a 24x7 basis to your visitors, if any problems arise with the property
- Demand: Tourist demand is the determining factor for the rental accommodation's popularity and quality.
- Seasonality: The demand for your property in a northern climate will probably drop drastically in winter (unless you reserve a ski chalet). In comparison, demand for rentals in colder southern locations (such as Arizona) decreases significantly in summer.

The places with the highest rent return are:

- In sought-after destinations where hotel prices are high (popular neighborhoods on Airbnb searches rank higher)
- Centrally located, near the tourist attractions, shops, and public transit
- It provides panoramic views and facilities such as balconies, car parks, etc.

3. What are your Economic Objectives? Looking to make some money at the side or produce steady income? Your business plan's financial portion will reflect target market analysis as well as reasonable projections of the potential revenue from renting your land.

Revenue from an Airbnb rental depends on:

Before you entertain thoughts about quitting your job and living by running an Airbnb company, make sure you look carefully at your property's income potential by looking at rental rates and booking frequencies for comparable Airbnb listings in your region.

4.Additional costs: Apart from the booking fees paid by Airbnb, there are other costs related to hosting on Airbnb, including

- **Insurance**

The insurance policies of typical homeowners do not include the use of the property for commercial purposes, which provides for renting on Airbnb. Airbnb provides a free Host Compensation Insurance program in the U.S., Canada, the U.K., and several other countries that offers up to $1 million in compensation against bodily injury or property damage. If Airbnb insurance does not cover your venue, contact an insurance agent for proper coverage.

- **Business Licenses:**

Airbnb hosts are increasingly being required by cities to possess a business license.

- **Cleaning and Repairing:**

To keep your Airbnb host rating secure, you need to keep your rental property in the top-rated list at all times, which includes thorough cleaning between visits to the guests and regular maintenance. If the cleaning and maintenance duties are to be subcontracted, the costs will add to your expenses.

- **How to Become an Airbnb Host?**

Okay, it is unbelievably easy.

- Only add to Airbnb
- Account verification and ID

- Tap "Become a Host" button
- Add to new listing.
- Take good shots of the place
- Fill in an eye-catching summary and list the available facilities
- That is, it! Get those $$s, it is as easy as creating a new profile on social media.

Now, these are a few key points that make the difference between someone competent on Airbnb and others who are not.

## 5.4 How to be a Successful Airbnb Host?

- Capture High-Quality Photos: Most people are going to browse through the listings, and if your place's pictures look dull, the chances of clicking through them are pretty low.
- Know your guest and have a USP (Only Selling Proposal): You need something special to make you stand out from all the other competitors in your region.
- Consider your potential guest and plan your explanation for them: is it known to be baby if you put it best for families? Remember that.
- Do you want short term tenants or people booking at least one month? You can increase the rates and give monthly tenants better discount percentages, so you don't have to deal with new guests every single day.
- Tell your guests to try this out. Reviews play a significant role in Airbnb's rankings, so if you can over deliver on your listing and have an excellent stay for your guests, they'll be more than happy to give you a useful review.
- **Higher Host Rankings**
  - Airbnb ratings are like internet search ratings–the higher your property shows in the rankings, the more likely visitors are to pick it, so getting top Airbnb

rankings is crucial to your Airbnb business ' success. You will boost your rankings by building confidence and by giving your visitors a great experience.

- **Building Rapport**
  - The community of Airbnb is built on trust, so guests can search for hosts that have checked contact information, references, and positive reviews.
  - Verification: Verification is particularly crucial for new hosts. It is updating your profile to include additional data such as your cell number, email id, Facebook profile, etc. to give potential guests some confidence that you are a trustworthy host.
  - References: References from friends, relatives, colleagues, business associates, etc. can be posted to create more trust. You will compose recommendations for other guests of Airbnb too.
- **Services**

Customer service, as any entrepreneur would tell you, is the cornerstone of any successful business, and being an Airbnb host is no different. Positive comments, higher search rankings, and more booking orders are awarded to Airbnb hosts who provide the best guest experience. The host with the most performance is:

When we choose a house, the response time to cleanliness is a close second. There is nothing worse than to book a hotel and having to wait 24 + hours for a host to determine if you can stay at their house.

Lastly, the thing you want to do is have your visitors in a dirty bathroom. Make sure it's safe, as the same thing you'd like. Just like in the kitchen, you want the bathroom to provide some essential items. Not only are there other criteria for the Airbnb host, but it's also common courtesy.

Here's a quick bathroom checklist for Airbnb properties:

- Bath towels (at least two)
- Paper towels (at least two)
- Additional toilet paper, and make sure it's in a prominent place
- Hand soap, and buy rechargeable bottles to save time
- Kleenex
- Hairdryer

I've seen some hosts include shampoo or body wash. That's good to have, but not necessarily. Many properties we have often stayed at have to use travel size bottles leftover from previous guests. While not part of the toilet, visitors will also need to be supplied with extra pillows, sheets, and hangers.

Airbnb understands this and provides all hosts with feedback ratings. In your response time, you want to strive for perfection since this can affect feedback. Hosts who can't be bothered with responding to inquiries in a timely fashion (or at all) are a big guest turnoff. Airbnb keeps track of your guest's responses and rates them accordingly. Hosts that have the best response scores are compensated with improved search rankings and bookings. The Airbnb mobile app is always able to help keep you connected. When visitors are present, be available by phone at all times and be open to them during extended stays to check if there is anything else you can do to improve the service.

- **Update Calendars Regularly**

Having your calendar updated enhances your Airbnb search rankings, as well as improving the guest experience.

- Repair any issues ASAP: If a guest mentions an item such as a leaky tap or burnt-out light bulb, get it fixed immediately and apologize to the guest. Five-star service is a sure way to improve the scores.

- Act on Their Reviews: If a guest posts a negative review to correct the problem, and learn from your errors. Each time, answer complaints professionally.
- **Get Insurance**

Airbnb provides the homeowners with up to $1,000,000 of insurance cover for loss or damage caused by theft or vandalism incurred by an Airbnb guest. But this isn't taking the place of insurance for homeowners or landlords. Always ensure you have adequate coverage, check your policy with your insurance carrier. Securing valuables in a safe and keeping clothes in a separate locked closet would also be sensible.

- **You may Comply with Your Homeowners**

They can ban short-term rentals from being subletted or restricted. If necessary, consult with your landlord. You may also think of adding a rider to your Airbnb rental agreement, which answers certain parties ' issues and outlines all involved obligations and liabilities.

- **Involve Your Neighbors**

Try notifying your hosting plans to neighbors or the doorman along with your policy to ensure that your visitors don't get disruptive. Sure, they may object to that. But if you ask for their help, they could be a lot more helpful and keep an eye on things.

- **Find Long-term Guests**

You can set a minimum duration of stay for 2 or 3 days. Only one night is not enough. You don't want to be a hotelier, work with transients, or deal with key sometimes.

- **You should not be Too Quick to Turn On Instant Book**

The' Instant Book ' functionality on Airbnb is close to the minimum night stay requirement. If you use the app' Instant Book,' it allows visitors to book your property without first contacting you.

It may be an excellent feature for you, but it may not work for others. Instant Book' helps you to get more last-minute bookings, but it also ensures you will not be able to screen visitors. You just know what's right for your needs. If you find it essential to be available to more last-minute bookings,' Instant Book' can be a useful tool to use.

- **A Separate Entrance**

It is directly applicable to Airbnb hosts who also reside at the house. We stayed at homes where the host lives, and you've got to enter through their front door. It may lead to a variety of problems, and those you certainly want to prevent. When you live in the house, you are listing, and you want a separate entrance to the house. It makes it easier for your visitors to get in. It also makes it easier for you as the host because it removes the need to think about when the guest arrives.

- **You can have a Key Code Entrance**

When you adhere to any of my hosting tips for Airbnb, it's this-have a key code entry to your house. It not only makes it easier for visitors to enter, but you can even use systems that allow you to see when you enter the code. When the guest walks in the door, you can see also. Most key code locks require you to reset the key code after every guest, so no security concerns. An entry to crucial code is a must-have. You want to have the access code issued within 24 hours of the guest's stay.

That way, they have the code, and when they arrive, they don't have to call you. But don't stop there just as critical is that you have a well-lit entrance. Your guest may arrive late at night, and as a guest, nothing is more frustrating than using a minimally lighted keypad. I suggest a light with motion sensing that gives enough light for entering the code. Once guests carry their bags in for the night, adequate lighting always helps.

For instance, we arrived after 1:00 am at the estate. Due to proper lighting, there was no question before and after. We all also may have experienced to come at properties just after dark and had difficulty because the host had little to no lighting outside. It may sound like a small point, but in a review, you never know what someone is going to leave. Also, the comments affect possible future guest decisions.

- **Walk Your Guests through Everything**

It's possibly one of the most ignored items on my checklist for the Airbnb hosting, but you want to clarify all of it to your guest. Think of this as a manual for your house, answering any question about your property they may have. Before a stay, we had hosts email us guidance. We had email reminders for hosts before a visit, too. That's nice, but at your place where you attend guests, you want to send written instructions. That can be as basic as a printed sheet, or in a notebook, it can be several sheets. We've both seen, and both work great–just make sure it's visible when you arrive.

- **Make Your Guests Feel Home**

Visitors who feel at home are more likely to leave positive reviews and become frequent visitors. You can do two main things to make them feel right at home. First of all, teach them about the environment around your property or town as a whole. Tell them about fashionable restaurants, resorts and places that you enjoy visiting. You want to include this in your written instructions and is a great way to help them understand their surroundings. Second, consider providing a couple of small snacks or bottles of water upon arrival. It can be as basic as several small trail mix bags, granola or protein bars, or a couple of small chip bags.

- **Get the Security Deposit**

Your homeowner's insurance is extremely likely not to cover short term rentals.

You may find a separate business strategy, but first, check your town regulations. Airbnb lets you charge $100 to $5,000 in a refundable security deposit. The deposit will only be used if the guest at your property damages an object. When they break it, Airbnb refunds the deposit after the stay. If they do break something, indeed, they use the funds to repair the object. Having separate savings account to cover things that you need to improve by normal wear and tear is also useful.

- **Better Communication is Always Fascinating**

You will think it's good for guests to "book your listing instantly." It streamlines the booking process after all and doesn't compel visitors to make a booking order. The instant book trait can mean more bookings for you as a host, but adding an extra communication layer to the booking process can give you some control over who is booking your listing and why. Its feature can be disabled and turned off as host wishes.

Many hosts prefer seeing the profile of a prospective guest and reading their reviews before approving a stay. They want to make sure that they know who is staying at their listing and that the guest's expectations are appropriate for the room. We also welcome a message from the prospective guest, which explains their reason for the stay. Clear communication before arrival is a reliable indicator of a good guest. Just as we advise guests to contact hosts before booking, a great host will respond to guests promptly and will be personable in their response. Most well-reviewed hosts are prompt with their responses and have a friendly tone.

Hosts should also be clear and straightforward when communicating on expectations, total costs, and check-in and check-out procedures to lessen any problems that may arise.

It is equally important to keep all contact with guests inside Airbnb and never agree to rent outside the network as you would not be eligible for a host guarantee from Airbnb (property damage insurance up to $1 million) if an unfortunate incident happened with a guest.

- **Decide on Cancellation Policy**

When choosing your cancelation policy, there are three levels: versatile, moderate, and stringent. I lived in over 100 Airbnb listings and was extremely fortunate that within a few days of check-in, a host never canceled me. The truth is cancelations are a common occurrence for both guests and hosts alike. As a host, a flexible cancelation policy (guests can cancel 24 hours before a stay) means a last-minute cancelation by a visitor, and you're scrambling for that planned stay to fill in the vacancy or lose revenues.

On the other end of the picture, a strict cancelation policy for a host means you are only entitled to refund the cost of the cleaning fee. Such a strict cancelation policy can offset a guest when they need flexibility with their travel plans. Hosts offer full or partial refunds to guests on a case-by-case basis outside the Airbnb policy cancelation window at their discretion. For example, if you have a strict cancelation policy but an imminent guest writes you three days before arrival that they have died in the family and are not going to stay on your listing anymore, you can give them a full refund. Determine can cancelation policy is best for you and allow for a little wiggle room to mitigate circumstances. Remember, you deal with people.

- **Aim for Airbnb Super-Host Status**

After you've become an Airbnb host and got into the hosting groove, you may wonder what the criteria are for earning the highly coveted super host status designation. After all, as a Super host, when guests perform a search, you receive priority placement, higher occupancy rates than non-Super hosts, and 60 percent more revenue per available day. As the name suggests, the top hosts on Airbnb are the Super hosts. Not only are they trustworthy and secure, but they are also always professional, and are known for their excellent customer service.

For achieving a super host status, the following criteria are required:

- You should complete at least ten trips OR complete three reservations totaling at least 100 nights
- Maintain a response rate of 90 percent or higher
- Maintain a cancelation rate of 1 percent (one cancelation per 100 reservations) or lower, with exceptions made for those protected by Airbnb's Extenuating Circumstances Policy
- Maintain You can apply for super host status if you fulfill the program requirements on the date of the quarterly assessment. Annual, quarterly reviews start January 1, April 1, July 1, and October 1. After each appraisal period, Airbnb will inform you of your super host status— which usually ends ten days after evaluation begins. Each host will strive for the state of a super host if they are serious about getting constant income from hosting their place.
- There are many Benefits of Having a Property Manager on Airbnb
- **Professional Listing:** Despite increasing numbers of properties appearing on Airbnb every day, a persuasive listing is essential. Airbnb property managers can provide tips on copywriting, photography, and interior design to

help you sing and improve bookings at your house. A qualified listing increases property efficiency and holds the occupancy high.

- **Monitoring and Support:** Guest monitoring, booking management, price monitoring, and minor maintenance and repairs are just a few of the many things Airbnb property managers can do.
- **Housekeeping:** Cleaning between guests is one of the activities that an Airbnb host will perform most of the time. Getting a property manager who can supervise washing and linen, restocking supplies, and professional cleaners make hosting stress-free.
- **Better Time and Asset Management:** For those among you with more than one Airbnb home, the responsibilities of managing and maintaining each property begin to add up. Hiring a specialist to handle your assets gives you the confidence that your property will always be ready and available for reservations, even if you are unable to arrange it.

## 5.5 Types of Hosts on Airbnb

There are reasons for several reasons why somebody would want to become an Airbnb entrepreneur — or a re-entrepreneur, as James and Symon call it.

- **The Opportunistic**

Generally, these are people who have some extra space in their current home or apartment, such as a spare bedroom or a guest casita, and who want to make some extra money. I also have specific times to pay and don't want to rent. For instance, when major sporting events such as the Super Bowl come to Phoenix, opportunists might open up some listings to capitalize on that.

- **Side-Hustle Seekers**

We work in a gig-economy. People drive to Uber and offer take-out through Grub hub, everything to make some extra cash. Side hustle hunters use Airbnb as a way of delivering secure extra income, but it's not a full-time gig. There may be occasions when they don't have a listing, but renting them out is relatively consistent. We, too, like the opportunist, would take advantage of special events.

- **The Full-time Re-entrepreneurs**

James and Symon describe renters as people who have at least one short-term rental property on Airbnb committed to full time. They want their primary income to be from short-term rentals, and they have plans to develop a whole portfolio. Full-time entrepreneurs realize that they need to concentrate on optimizing the potential profit from every hour they spend hosting their company, not just profit per unit. Before you start your Airbnb business, it's essential to know your why because it will inform your approach. All of them are substantial grounds for opting into Airbnb, but only one of them will make you productive: the full-time renter.

- **Measures Taken to Provide Safety to Host**

We put hosts and guests on watch lists for authorities, threats, and sanctions. And they are also performing background checks for hosts and guests in the United States. When booking, each guest is requested to provide Airbnb with their full name, date of birth, photo, phone number, email address, and payment details. Home hosts also have the option of asking guests to send a government ID to Airbnb before booking their listing.

It can also be helpful to read feedback from that guest's previous bookings and what other hosts say about their stay with them.

These reviews can only be added after the booking has been completed; therefore, they are based on experience. Before it is confirmed, every Airbnb reservation is rated for danger. They use predictive analytics and machine learning to quickly analyze hundreds of signals helping to detect and investigate suspicious activity before it happens. And their customer service is in 11 languages, available 24/7.

# Chapter 6: How to List on Airbnb?

A new Airbnb or short-term rental company will yield social capital and financial capital, of course–both without actually needing any investment at your end. There are a variety of roads you can go down to achieve success with Airbnb and optimize the advantages of property management, and they all start by publishing your first list. Here's a step-by-step method for taking you through the design cycle and perfecting your first listing from start to finish. There is no need to get frustrated-the hard part is to build your listing. Once the listing has been completed and released, you can give us the keys to push your Airbnb listing towards more bookings, with hands-off account management in no small measure.

## 6.1 How to Do Listing on Airbnb?

- **Get Start**

First things first: go to airbnb.com and choose the option' add the listing' at the top right corner of the homepage. You will be provided with a form that prompts you to fill out your place's most general requirements. Remember that only after creating an account can you complete this first step, so it may be more convenient to sign up (or login) before you start. If you have not yet logged in, then at this point you will be prompted to enter your details.

- **Type of Home**

Such choices are relatively straightforward and include a whole house, private room, or shared room. Choose the option which best describes the property you manage.

The distinction is one of the most important because both you and your guests can be precise about preserving a certain level of privacy. So, make sure you construct your listing correctly to attract the most suitable guests for your house. Consider the fact that giving visitors full access to your listing can require access to other facilities on the property, such as a pool house or garage, before selecting "Entire place." Additionally, the "Private Home" option provides more home-sharing than you would normally expect, such as standard rooms, bathrooms, or kitchens.

- **Number of Guests**

The checklist allows you to pick the maximum number of people within your listing that can comfortably fit. For the time being, measure how many guests you can provide if each has its bed, sofa bed, or inflatable mattress, so the sleep arrangement is as convenient as you would imagine if you were the guest yourself. Lastly, select the appropriate number from the specified drop-down list.

- **City Name**

When you start typing your town name, Airbnb will automatically recommend all appropriate matches. Allow the option accordingly. Based on your listing form, guest ability, and venue, Airbnb will give you an estimate of how much you can earn per month at this point. Click the' Start' button and proceed to Step 1. You will be asked for the provision of more specific details about your listing here. Next, from a list that includes apartment, home, secondary unit, unique room, bed and breakfast, and boutique hotel, you must pick the most accurate description of your property type. You will need to choose a more specific explanation from a second drop-down menu once you've selected your listing type.

For instance, if you have described your listing as a' Unique Space,' you will need to specify further whether it is a barn, an igloo, a tent, or one of several other choices. The menu will appear for you to fill out based on your preferences. When you move on, you'll provide more detail on your page, including the number of beds and toilets, the exact address, and the facilities that you're offering. You must select the right facilities for your Airbnb.

Each segment has a long list of features ranging from standard rooms or extra rooms to home security measures. You are only provided the option to choose from the available list of facilities at this point in the listing. Still, once the listing has been done, you will be able to edit this part and add some new or further explanations and information. Make sure to include any correct feature as some guests may be influenced by specific features or become uninterested because of a lack of them. You can provide this guide for the basics that every host should include to optimize an Airbnb experience if you're lost in here. When an incorrect listing secures a booking, you will not be able to change the flawed conditions for that listing without first submitting a request for modification to the guest concerned. It might cost you a reservation and waste your time. So be careful with the specifics of your listing, because even a small error can have a considerable impact. Please remember that you can go back to edit the descriptions given above at any point. You'll upload photos of your property in this phase, write a brief description of the location and improve your Airbnb SEO data. Instead, remind potential guests how much you will be available during their stay, what they can expect from the area, and how they can get around town.

- **Show Casing the Scenery**

Photos: Regardless of how many you choose to add, the first three are the most relevant as they represent the view into your listing before users decide to click on the status or not. It is the most reason to offer high-quality and standout photos. Try taking this opportunity to show off restaurants, funky rooms, or other unique features of your house. For better resolution, Airbnb suggests using larger images (1024x 683px) and even offers free professional photography sessions to help you capture your location.

Description: The key attributes of your listing in 250 characters or less are described in an excellent summary. Customers like a bit of personality, so let yours shine and clarify what makes your place special. Too much writing looks overwhelming, so try to break it up; it can go a long way with bullet points and short sentences. You'll get a name for your page too. Think of your first experience of the story. You want to make those 35 characters captivating enough to catch attention and unique enough to represent your location with precision. Consider cushioning the title with concise and friendly adjectives. You will then add a photo of yourself to give the guests an idea of who will host them.

- **Becoming Ready for the Guests**

The final section is divided into three parts: Calendar, Booking Settings, and Price.

- **Calendar**

To get started, you will be able to select how often you would like to have visitors at your house, how often notice you will need before your guests arrive, how much time in advance they can book your place and how long they will stay.

Then you would be able to flip through your calendar manually and block or unblock specific dates or even whole months. The unique rental dates available should be entered as soon as you post your listing and should be regularly updated.

- **Booking Settings**

In this portion, you can review the basic guest requirements of Airbnb and may choose to make additional criteria such as having a government-issued ID and other hosts ' recommendations and zero negative reviews. You will then set the rules for your house and provide essential details about your home, such as whether visitors need to climb stairs or find their parking.

- **Pricing**

Pricing is always tricky, no matter what business. You want to choose a fair price that will not drive away potential guests but also allow you to make a good profit.

The pricing should be consistent with other similar listings in your region and should reflect some of the following:

- Location
- Amenities provided
- If it is a weekday or weekend stay

Airbnb provides it's Smart Pricing ' function to assist you with pricing. You can use this method to decide a fair, competitive price when making your listing. You don't have to use it, but when you start as an Airbnb host, it can be useful. Airbnb will give you the option to use their Smart Pricing tool, which will change your prices automatically according to fluctuations in demand in your region.

You will then be required to set a base price for which Airbnb will recommend an estimate based on the information you have received up to now, as well as patterns that currently affect the local rental market, such as holidays, increased tourism, and more. Remaining relevant and competitive is crucial, so be sure to compare the prices of similar Airbnb listings in your region. You'll then set a minimum amount, a maximum price, and the currency you'd like to charge your guests in. Your research on similar listings should also give you an idea of how to price your listing. It must be competitively priced to keep your property regularly booked (and optimize the profits).

In addition to general listing qualities and market activity, there are several other factors to consider when determining a price. For one, you might want to exercise your right to adjust the current rates for your listing by developing weekly or monthly packages to promote longer rents. It would help if you also were taking into account the cost of electricity, taxes, or early cleaning–Airbnb also gives you the option of adding a cleaning fee to the bill. It is worth noting that while these cannot be included in a basic rate, fines for late check-in or other unique factors should be reported before a reservation is obtained. The last move in the price section will be to decide for or against such deals, such as a 20 percent discount for your first three customers to help you attract visitors and get some initial good reviews for your listing. You can also offer weekly or monthly discounts for guests booking longer stays.

- **Publish Your Listing**

You're able to publish on Airbnb after you've done all of this. It is when you are pleased with your listing. One thing to remember is always to be frank about your explanation. When the guests arrive, it won't take long for the truth to come out. Nonetheless, trying to spin all of the aspects of your position in a constructive light as possible will be beneficial to you.

Now I am very hopeful that you would have grasped a lot about Airbnb re-renting and earnings. In this chapter the most important factor listing is discussed. It is worth reading as everything needed from start to end of a guest's tour is described thoroughly. But, still, I consider that there is a need to give you some more food for learning. So, in the coming chapters, I will share more about passive earning on Airbnb and what are its pros and cons. You will also be in condition to know your responsibilities as a host on Airbnb.

# Chapter 7: Some More Secretes Revealing that Airbnb Rentals are an Ultimate Passive Income Source

We're talking a lot about at the side making money. Some people want extra money, but they think they need specialized skills. Thankfully that is not the case. In reality, one of the great ways to make extra money is to use readily available tools, like a spare room in your home. You can use it to make money with Airbnb if you have an extra bedroom. Airbnb is a service that helps people to avoid expensive hotels by staying at a more inexpensive rental for the short term. When on holiday, my family and I often live in Airbnb properties. It allows us to save time, will enable us to cook our meals, and has a homier atmosphere compared to staying at a hotel.

The best part about making money with Airbnb is that the income is relatively passive. Passive income needs little or no effort and allows you to create multiple income streams.

Several sources of income support in achieving many financial goals, such as:

• Debt offsetting faster

• Supplementing certain savings

• Financing travel plans

• Planning for a significant expense

If you have a second property or spare room, you don't use and want to know how to make money with Airbnb without owning property, and this post outlines the steps needed to create a passive income source. As we will be addressing, it is possible to make a monthly listing of your property on Airbnb at $1,000+. It provides an excellent way to make money yourself and add to your profits.

- **What Percentage Does Airbnb take from the Profit?**

Now that we know how to make money from Airbnb, it is essential to understand how Airbnb is trying to make money from it. While it is free to list your property on Airbnb, Airbnb charges you three percent of the profits every time your property is booked. The three percent is taken out of your gross payout and helps make a profit for the Airbnb site.

- **Receiving Payment**

Airbnb issues payment 24 hours after checking in at your hotel.

- ACH / Direct Deposit: up to three business days
- Bank or international wire transfer: three to seven business days
- PayPal: during one business day
- Western Union: one business day
- Pioneer Prepaid Debit Card: within one business day as you can see, Airbnb allows payment relatively easy.

## 7.1 Who Uses Airbnb?

We usually use Airbnb for holidays. For most hosts, the industry is built on that.

There are many other reasons why a person or family may choose to stay at a short-term rental rather than a hotel, such as:

- Extended stay to visit a sick friend or family member
- Visit your town to attend a business conference, concert or sporting event
- Having a place that includes a kitchen
- Having a home with laundry facilities on site
- Saving money on travel as you can see, there are many reasons for this. It provides ample space for Airbnb to make money.

- **Yes! Making Money with Airbnb Re-Rentals is a Passive Income**

Passive Profit is the holy grail of new money-making. Earning extra money on the side is a great thing to do, but many side hustles allow you to make it possible with your time or effort. Often, that is not the case with Airbnb making money. Indeed, being an Airbnb host is one of the best ideas for seeking passive income. The research and promotion behind attracting guests are primarily done through the Airbnb website. There's also little need for routine maintenance with an Airbnb house. After each visit, you still have to clean the house, but that's also something you can contract out to minimize the need for work further. If you want to make money with Airbnb, using a spare room or second property and building a passive income stream can be a great way to. Would you think you can make money with Airbnb? It allows you to make the minimum effort to earn cash and augment your earnings. What other passive revenue sources do you pursue? Would you ever consider renting a spare room at a stranger's house?

## 7.2 Here Are Some Tips for Success When You are on Airbnb Rentals

Saving for retirement may sound like a difficult task. Investors need to be actively involved in their retirement plan to build a proper nest egg, and one way to earn stable, long-term income is through investment in land. Holiday rentals properties are a great way to earn passive revenue. Airbnb properties make substantial investments for your portfolio, and investors in real estate will expect an excellent return on their capital over time.

You cannot just buy any house, of course, and hope it will work out.

Property investment can be pricy, but you can use Airbnb rentals to protect your retirement if you play your cards correctly. If you're considering holiday rental income, here are some tips for making money from your investment in Airbnb. Now you will be well familiar that Airbnb is a platform where individuals rent a property or spare rooms. Airbnb itself takes approximately 3 percent of the host's booking fee and a small percentage of visitors. Such properties can be as basic as space or as expansive as a whole home. The goal is to give potential renters unused space with facilities to build up extra revenue. Property owners put rules in place to show what their rent provides, and visitors book it like a hotel. If you're considering this as a long-term investment, here are some tips to help you make it work.

- **Scope Up the Property**

The Airbnb property only matters where you own it. Tourists are outstanding, steady income, and potential tourists are always on the lookout for a place to stay in for a bargain. It, of course, depends on where people go, who they bring with them and what they expect to do. You want a "healthy bones" position, which will also take very little to maintain.

The first step if you want to cash in on your rental property is to find out the best locations. You'll probably do better with beach properties and homes in the vicinity of new appointments than something two-three hours away from any points of interest.

One of the property's key selling points is how that looks! Customers won't rent a dump, so reviews are essential. The aim is to make your rental property a place people want to stay in. Don't just make it livable; create a space that tourists want to return to, and that means keeping up with your rental's repairs, upkeep, and general look.

- **Select a Place Having Accessibility to Everything Easily**

Location is again one of the most significant factors when choosing a home. It's not only necessary to pick an option near a place of interest, but you also have to make sure it's close to the action! It doesn't have to be a property right in front of the beach but scope your choices.

Citizens on holiday wish to stay close to everything. Keeping it in mind, people who are away from home, on business or for fun will know what is happening around them and have easy access to all. For example, it may be perfect for passive income to have a rental space near major convention halls for business travelers. Choose the place you rent wisely!

- **Have Positive Reviews**

People thrive on reviews in the Age of information. Social media can make your property or ruin it, and you can bet your rent would make it on one of the biggest channels. Allow your Instagram able rental enough for photos with cute choices in decor and furniture. In reality, getting professional photographs taken is one of the best ways of selling your potential tourists. Combined with a good location, outstanding maintenance, and that extraordinary hospitality, you want your guests everywhere to leave rave reviews. Also, you want to make sure that your communication lines are available, and that your instructions and goals are transparent. Miscommunication is a simple means of getting a bad review.

- **Keep Things Clean**

It is an easy, but essential tip; keep clean your rental property. Tidy up regularly, thoroughly scrub, and keep the yard in order. Anyone would not want to rent a dirty house, fitting in with many of the previous points.

Besides, it's expected to produce bad reviews if you are to hold the property up. It is not worth renting properties if they don't generate a profit. If you're worried about keeping your property safe, be sure to set the rules up front, such as whether you tolerate rental pets, smoking, or other behaviors. Adding additional home insurance is a must for covering yourself. Take steps to provide legal protection against fraud, theft, and any unwanted guests in the building.

## 7.3 How is Airbnb Different from Traditional Renting?

Instead of conventional renting, there are considerable advantages to renting by Airbnb, but there can also be some drawbacks. Determining where or when to rent a vacation home is no longer the main challenge for families moving around. Today, it can be a problem with how to rent a house. Should you go online through a conventional rental agency or new direct bookings?

- **How Airbnb Works?**

On Airbnb, travelers directly rent from the owner of the property, which can allow more flexibility on both sides. Hosts in more than 190 countries rent out rooms, entire homes, and even castles. The traveler searches for locations, host profiles, and reviews of properties. The traveler can then contact a host after creating a profile and request a reservation. Many hosts tend to have a consultation at Airbnb with prospective guests before approving or rejecting an application, while others will make instant bookings. Travelers are also welcome to ask the host's questions and to sort out any dates or particular request information.

- **How Traditional Rental Agencies Work?**

A traveler opts for a town and then finds a rental agency in that town. The traveler is not dealing directly with the property owner. Usually, the rental agent can answer any questions or be the middleman between the owner and the traveler. The traveler may be able to search for properties online or may have the opportunity to visit the property in person with a rental agent if the place is close to home. Most traditional holiday properties are limited to the specific timeframe of travel dates, and can often only require week-long reservations.

- **Airbnb Payment**

Upon approval of the reservation, visitors usually have two options: they can pay upfront the total cost or pay half at the time of booking and the remainder at the time of stay. As the date of travel approaches, arrangements are made between the traveler and the host. It is done for check-in and check-out and how to pick up the key. Contact information for the host is also provided. Travelers are recommended to be respectful of the neighbors ' home and considerate (but of course, mostly encouraged to have fun).

- **Traditional Vocation Agencies Payments**

Most rental agencies require a deposit upon reservation, and the balance is due as the date of travel approaches. Coming in and check-out times are set by the department and are often strictly enforced to allow turnover cleaning times. The contractor often predetermines the essential details, and sometimes enable the traveler to pick up and drop the key at the office of the rental management company. Often travelers can be given a welcome bag or packet with information about the region, too.

- **Airbnb Refunds**

If a guest encounters a travel problem or the holiday home rental does not meet Airbnb requirements by failing to fit the online description, a refund may be requested if the issuer complies with the Guest Refund Policy. If the holiday home is not in the specified venue, does not have the facilities mentioned, is not generally clean, or is not the size described, the guest may be given a refund at the discretion of Airbnb.

- **Traditional Rental Agencies Refunds**

Many agencies have 30-, 60- or 90-day cancelation plans that are strictly enforced, and deposits can be reimbursed within those timeframes. Because the department inspected the properties, it is doubtful that any property surprises would be faced upon arrival by travelers.

- **Airbnb Reviews**

Travelers are encouraged to revisit the property and host after a visit, which may be helpful when making travel arrangements for the next guest. Sometimes, the host must test the renter, which might help or hinder your subsequent rental request, so make sure you're a welcome guest.

- **Traditional Rental Agencies Reviews**

Most rental agencies may be able to post reviews online, but not all of them do. The department will take into consideration any grievances and ideally relay them directly to the property owner.

## 7.4 What are the Advantages and Disadvantages of Airbnb?

- **Advantages of Airbnb**

Hosts don't have to pay to list the properties. Listings can include written explanations, captioned images, and a user profile where potential guests can get to know the hosts a little bit. Participating in Airbnb for hosts is a way to earn some money from their house, but with the possibility that the guest will ruin it. The benefit can be relatively inexpensive rooms for visitors, but with the chance that the property will not be as appealing as the listing made it appear.

- **Free Listings**

Airbnb hosts list several different types of property on the Airbnb website — single rooms, a suite of apartments, condos, moored yachts, houseboats, whole homes, even a castle.

- **Hosts May Set Your Price**

It is up to each host to decide how much to charge each night, week, or month.

Hosts can be extremely welcoming.

- **Hosts have Inside Knowledge**

Hosts have extensive field expertise. Best restaurants, games, etc. Imagine these as your concierge.

- **Customizable Searches**

Guests can check the Airbnb website - not only by date and location, but also by price, property type, amenities, and the host language. There are also additional services.

Airbnb has increased its facilities in the last few years to include activities and cafes.

In addition to a list of available hotels for the dates they plan to travel, a list of activities, such as classes and sightseeing, provided by local Airbnb hosts will be shown to people searching by location. Airbnb host's comments are also included on restaurant lists.

- **Protection for Guests and Hosts**

Airbnb keeps the payment of the guest for 24 hours after check-in, before transferring the funds to the host, as guest security.

For hosts, the Airbnb Host Guarantee policy "provides protection to protected property in the rare event of guest injury, in qualifying countries, for up to $1,000,000 in damages."

- **Disadvantages of Airbnb**
- **You May Not Get What You See**

Booking Airbnb accommodation is not like booking a room with a major hotel chain, where you have fair guarantees that the property will be as advertised. Individual hosts make their lists, and some may be more honest than others. Past participants, however, also post comments about their experiences, which can provide a more objective perspective.

- **There are Chances of Potential Damage**

Probably the most significant risk to hosts is that it will harm their house. While most stays go without a problem, there are reports that hundreds of party-goers were trashing entire houses when the Airbnb owners thought they were renting to a peaceful couple. Airbnb's host guarantee program, as we have described earlier, provides some assurance but may not cover everything like cash, rare artwork, jewelry, and pets. Hosts whose homes are damaged can also encounter significant inconvenience.

- **Added Fees**

Airbnb implements several additional fees (as do hotels and other suppliers of accommodation, of course). In addition to the reservation fee, visitors pay a guest service charge of 0 percent to 20 percent to cover customer support and other services provided by Airbnb. Prices appear in the currency chosen by the customer, provided Airbnb sponsors it. Banks or issuers of credit cards that charge additional fees, if applicable. And while rentals are free, Airbnb charges for hosting a service fee of at least 3 percent for each booking, for covering the transaction processing expense.

- **You have to Face Taxes**

The value-added tax (VAT) can apply to both hosts and guests from the European Union, Switzerland, and Norway. And the hosts may be subject to rental income taxes depending on their location. Airbnb collects taxpayer information from hosts to assist with U.S. tax compliance so they can give a report of their earnings each year via forms.

- **It is Not Legal Everywhere**

I have already told you about this but, let me remember it to you again. Until listing their property on Airbnb, would-be hosts need to review their local zoning regulations to make sure that renting out their properties is legal.

## 7.5 What are the Pros and Cons of Airbnb Rental Investments?

- **What are the Pros of Airbnb Rental Investments?**

Whether you've stayed for a vacation in an Airbnb rental, or just learned about the attractive possibilities of owning a sought-after short-term property, owning an Airbnb rental portfolio may seem like a smart way to boost your passive income.

Using the Airbnb platform to rent properties can be a profitable investment strategy in real estate— or a rival like VRBO or HomeAway, but it also poses challenges. In some situations, merely renting a property to a single occupant may be more comfortable and more profitable, or failing to invest completely for real estate.

Here are some of the main advantages and disadvantages of using Airbnb as an investment strategy, as well as short-term rentals.

- **Airbnb Rental Investment Maybe Lucrative Than Traditional Renting**

A decisively booked Airbnb rental could be more profitable than a single long-term tenant renting the same property. That's because, usually, you can charge more nightly.

For example, in Seattle, the average rent of apartments is about $2,000 per month. That would be $24,000 in gross income if the tenant signed a 12-month lease. But what if you have gone on the Airbnb way? According to AirDNA, on the average daily charges for an Airbnb rental in Seattle is around $150, and units are occupied an average of 270 days a year. If you rented out your Airbnb for $150 per night for a total of 270 nights of a year, you could take up to $40,500 in gross revenue from the rent. That is $16,000 more than traditional renting would make you. These figures only represent total revenue: If the value of the property appreciates, the actual revenue could be higher. The net income could also be much lower due to different land ownership and management expenses.

- **You will have a Diversified Portfolio of Tenants**

You are placing the eggs in a single basket with one tenant with conventional renting.

If the occupant is financially stable and stays for a long time, this can work fine. But if they ever miss rent payments or disappear in the night, your income takes an immediate hit, which is hard to replace immediately.

With an Airbnb rental, you frequently receive revenues from different tenants. -renter represents a tiny percentage of your total income, so if any of them cancel on payment at the last minute, or otherwise flake, it may not have a significant impact. Your dream of owning and renting an Airbnb property may never get off the ground, depending on where you live. Many jurisdictions have placed restrictions on investment rentals for Airbnb, making it almost impossible to rent out a property other than your own home.

For example, you can't rent out any part of a property in San Francisco unless it's your primary residence, defined as your stay on the property at least 275 nights a year. So holding more than 90 nights of "unhosted" rentals is illegal, meaning you aren't present when visitors are there. In many situations, such limitations have been implemented to ensure adequate accommodation for tenants. Still, they are likely to reduce potential earnings for someone who wants to make money from Airbnb.

- **Host Guarantee**

In the rare case of any incident that causes damage or injury, Airbnb has insurance programs that secure you and your house. When a guest makes a reservation and stays at your home, their Host Guarantee automatically covers you.

- **Home Insurance**

The host Coverage Insurance program offers up to $1 million per incident for primary liability coverage. The software protects against claims of liability occurring during a stay in a listing, or on an Airbnb property.

- **Experience Insurance**

Experience protection insurance provides hosts with free liability insurance of up to $1 million to protect against claims for personal injury or damage to property.

- **Expenses Maybe Higher**

If you have a property and rent it to a single tenant, your interaction with the property manager may be limited. A conscientious tenant will regularly pay bills, keep the site clean, mow the lawn, and store the cupboards. All you need to do is step in to perform property maintenance or handle the occasional emergency.

An Airbnb property is likely to be more labor-intensive, as it will fall on you, the owner, to ensure that the property is always in tip-top shape. There are also things that you probably will need to provide that you wouldn't usually offer to a single tenant, like:

- **High-Quality Furniture, Decor, Appliances and Amenities**

If you want to impress potential Airbnb tenants, you might need to invest some cash to make sure the location looks classy and feels good. Airbnb guests would like to feel like they're living in a high-end house.

- **Food**

You don't have to prepare food for your Airbnb guests, but keeping certain essential food items in the refrigerator can go a long way to keeping guests happy. Stocking of fresh eggs, coffee, or alcoholic beverages may be involved. Some Airbnb hosts also make a point of bringing snacks out at different times of the day.

- **Cable, TV, Wi-Fi, and Others**

It will usually be the duty of guest to hook up cable TV, Wi-Fi, login to Netflix, and so on when you rent to a single tenant. On the other hand, Airbnb renters usually expect these things to be in place during their stay, so the cost of this infrastructure – and maintenance – will fall to you. In hiring a cleaning company and property management firm to perform all of these duties, you may be able to save yourself time and work but would also add to your operating costs. Airbnb collects taxes on tourism and occupancy from renters in many locations and remits them to the appropriate taxing authorities. Many jurisdictions, however, allow you to pay some or all of the taxes manually.

- **What are the Cons of Airbnb Rental Investments?**
- **Possible Damage**

There is still a risk you can find harm that is not compensated by the Airbnb Insurance.

- **Success May Be Gradual**

It's doubtful from the beginning that you will be able to keep an Airbnb unit booked almost every night. Bookings via Airbnb derive primarily from your management credibility. The higher your past renter scores, the more likely you are to attract new ones. You may have very few reviews, in the beginning, so you may need to keep the rent prices low or offer incentives to keep people staying. Even if you're in a prime location with a fantastic house, don't assume you're going to bring in rental income instantly.

- **Income Maybe Irregular**

If you own a property and rent to a single landlord, you may be able to keep the landlord on a long-term lease and receive rent every month.

It can provide a steady stream of sales. Rentals with Airbnb may be much more variable. While you can rent a property 365 days a year in principle, there are many empty dates on your calendar that you will have. You may even choose to have a day or two empty between bookings to ready the property for the next visitor. In a post on the group message board of Airbnb, an owner named Michelle says that 60 percent of the time her properties are booked, depending on the season6. He said bookings drop to 40 percent during the wet season in New Orleans, but her rentals in Massachusetts are complete 75 percent during the busiest tourist seasons. "I have a total of three days, so I block a day between bookings," Michele wrote in the Airbnb update. "So there are delays of 1-3 days even in a' full' month that happen to fall between reservations. As a proprietor, by charging more than a typical rental unit, you may be able to offset these empty dates, but there's no guarantee that you'll be coming out ahead. We have discussed Airbnb rentals, what are the benefits of renting on Airbnb, and how one can earn passive income from the Airbnb platform. It will be apparent to you that for Airbnb rentals hosting is the main thing without which your plan will not flourish. Yes, you are thinking right. Airbnb hosting has a lot of benefits, but there are some cons too. Now It would be good to summarize them.

# Chapter 8: What are the Pros and Cons of Airbnb Hosting?

As Airbnb first launched, its mission was to provide home sharing in someone's home, either shared space or a private room. It was a wholly alien and almost crazy idea at first. The first short term rentals were vacation rentals, but Airbnb launched an entirely new concept. Would strangers come to your home and stay? It is crazy! Fast forward to 2018, and many Airbnb hosts are paying their rent and gaining money as travelers share their homes. There are still many people who are anxious about letting strangers into their intimate space: their house. Whether it's a holiday home, your spare bedroom, or your living room, there's money on Airbnb to make. As with any company, Airbnb has pros and cons for hosts. Becoming an Airbnb host has many advantages and is priceless. And since Airbnb continues to thrive as a useful tool for short-term rental owners to advertise their properties, there's no excuse you shouldn't join the bandwagon.

## 8.1 Pros of Airbnb Rental Hosting

If you are having a spare room in your house, the benefits are pretty logical to rent it out. First, you're going to make money reasonably passively, especially if you're not doing the self-cleaning. That could be a substantial amount of money, depending on your business. Some hosts that do rental arbitrage, who host short-term rentals in a home they rent on their own, actually make enough to cover their whole rent and more. Secondly, you will come across a lot of interesting people, and perhaps even make friends with them.

If you have or are planning to buy a holiday home, second home, or investment property, then it might be a wise choice to consider turning it into a short term rental.

Compared to a traditional long-term owner, short-term rentals usually generate much more gross revenue. You can easily take in more than double the rent, or more, depending on your business. In our market, in peak season, our houses make more than five times the monthly mortgage payment.

Many experienced hosts do not discuss it, but hosting is often a fun and rewarding experience. Hearing guests compliment your hospitality could do a great deal for your morale. Being a professional Airbnb host, being a landlord is an accelerated crash course.

- **There is More Flexibility**

One of the primary advantages of not having a long-term tenant in your home is the ability to block off dates that just don't have your home. By blocking dates on your Airbnb calendar, those dates become off-limits for any potential guest. Many scenarios where this is useful include: you expect to be out of town for a holiday and don't feel like having to worry about having any visitors at home that week. You've got friends coming to the city in a few months, and you'd like them to stay at your Airbnb home. You need to take care of a significant repair, but you'd rather wait a few weeks to pay to get the work done.

You would have no recourse in each of these cases if you were a traditional landlord, but all you would have to do as an Airbnb host is mark off whatever dates you want. It has been handy for us many times and is one of our favorite short-term vs. long-term rentals perks. My grandma came down from Missouri in September to spend the month here in Florida with us. She'd had to stay in a room in my parent's home in the past. But this year on Airbnb, we've just closed off the whole month of September. We had a great visit, and she loved being able to use an entire home while she was back!

- **More Control**

It could be my favorite advantage of taking the Airbnb path over being conventional landlords.

- **Control of Your Home's Look After**

Once you sign a lease with long-term tenants, you immediately lose much of your home power. They are the ones who live it day in and day out, and you get very few chances to see how well we look after your house. You would have heard many horror stories of homeowners who have discovered their home was trashed by their tenants and will have to make significant repairs before they can get ready for new renters. You can check your home regularly with Airbnb, usually every couple of days.

- **Control of How You Get Paid**

One of the things we love about Airbnb is that our guests have paid before they've ever stayed at our home. We never have to contend with the monthly tension that many landlords are trying to pursue tenants to collect their rent. We just love knowing we're never going to have to deal with the painful process of evicting someone from our house. There are times when being a landlord requires to have some pretty hard skin. If you do not think you have the type of personality to deal with the "Hey, give me my rent, or otherwise" side of being a landlord, that's okay. You can still earn income from your home with Airbnb, without having to deal with those particular issues.

- **There is More Revenue**

In one location, it would be about $1,300, about the average one might expect to get for a two-bedroom, two-bath house with conventional rent.

Yet in the summer, they may have won $3,700 during their best month. That is almost twice the salary! We all know that for a week-long stay in a hotel, we often pay nearly as much as for our month-long mortgages or rental payments. Why not take advantage of that to your position? If you're in an area where there's enough competition, you will undoubtedly make more money as an Airbnb host than you as a landlord can. The most apparent advantage of being an Airbnb host has extra revenue. Overall, a more significant income can be accrued than just having your pay. Several property owners found it lucrative that they had chosen to become full-time hosts. Your earning as a short-term rental owner will no doubt also depend on a lot of factors. Place, #of rooms available, public transport accessibility, and top attractions, and the overall effort you put in to produce an enjoyable experience will affect your earning potential. The cash stream from hosting would give you a daily (mostly passive) monthly income, enabling you to use your time any way you want. It contributes to an increase in revenue.

- **There is No Hard Work on Your End**

Because the benefits of becoming an Airbnb host are fantastic, your time, resources, and commitment are still needed. But the good news is you can opt-out of all the dirty work. Just bring it to Great residences.

Be completely fret-free, and just enjoy your incomes while we look after the rest. Our team manages everything for you from rental washing, key exchange, listing and promoting your Airbnb to hosting guests 24/7. While you're off to some tropical paradise worldwide, you can simply wait for the monthly check. That is not hype at all!

The benefits of being an Airbnb host were invaluable. It is particularly true because the demand for short-term rentals is likely to continue to expand.

But you should seriously consider hiring a full-service property management company to optimize its advantages to the maximum. With Great houses as your partner, you can be assured of receiving all these amazing benefits without the horrible tension!

- **You have an excellent opportunity for Learning New Skills**

Short term rental owners just by being an Airbnb host, pick up a lot of new skills. You will quickly build expertise in numerous areas such as customer service, marketing, communications, negotiations, finance, Airbnb listing optimization, and hosting and running a company, of course. And yes, you'll even learn something or two from guests staying at your rental unit. Each visitor you host is unique, whether they are foreigners or locals. There's a lot of cultures, histories, and life experiences that you might benefit from. All these things will, no doubt, help you and broaden your horizons.

- **When You are an Airbnb Host, you meet New People**

The advantage of becoming an Airbnb host is that you will have the opportunity to meet many interesting and adventurous people from all over the world — virtually and or in real life. Very positively, such guests would come from all walks of life, visiting your city for different reasons. Some may be business travelers attending a nearby conference. Others might be families with young children who are looking to explore a theme park in your city. Regardless of the type of visitors you invite to your rental home, one thing is for sure — if not for Airbnb hosting, you wouldn't have met them otherwise. If you have good luck, some guests even become regular guests, essential friendships, and even lifelong mates.

- **You can Diversify Your Investments**

You have probably invested money in the stock market or other real estate assets. Yet hosting Airbnb and short term rentals require a completely different environment compared to other forms of real estate. Now, if it's not even part of your investment portfolio, it can be a great way to get started in real estate. Plus, you'll also help protect your investment portfolio against market volatility by diversifying your investments.

- **You have Relaxation on Taxes Payment**

Possessing a rental property and being an Airbnb host means you have the right to substantial tax benefits and deductions. Second, the rental earnings over the short term are tax-free!

- Individual taxes you can write-off:
- Hypothecary interest
- Credit card interest in rental property sales
- Insurance
- Reparation payments and repairs
- Travel expenses
- Legal and professional fees
- Property tax

These tax rewards will no doubt enhance your income and ROI.

## 8.2 What are the Disadvantages of Airbnb Hosting?

Though Airbnb has many advantages and disadvantages, and the list of problems is much longer than the pros. Does this mean that the drawbacks outweigh the pros? Not! While this list will be long, but by no means comprehensive, it should not deter aspiring hosts. We want to brace you for challenges that you might face on your journey to Super host.

- **The danger of a Stranger, It Damages Liability and Squatters**

If you're planning to share a room in your home, or even just a shared space, it's essential to realize that screening that person will be up to you. Airbnb has a few options in place to help potential screen guests, but you may end up with some unpleasant guess that's just part of the business, there are pros and cons for hosts. Fortunately, as you become a more experienced host, you'll soon discover when to turn down a guest.

If you rent a whole listing, you're not going to have to deal directly with your guests, but they're going to be under less supervision. Most likely, they will destroy items, or get injured or even refuse to leave. While you are running a similar risk with a long-term rental, the chances are higher that you will run into this issue with Airbnb due to the volume of different people moving in and out of your list. Luckily, there is a Host Guarantee for Airbnb, as well as commercial insurance plans, and security deposits to have your back.

- **A Burden of Super host, it is a 24/7 Responsibility**

Being a professional Airbnb host often feels like you are on-call 24/7. Guest inquiries, questions, comments, and complaints will be addressed to all of you. You're being asked for discounts, complaining about everything under the sun, and quietly questioning how some people made it a past grade. It is likely to cause you to have flashbacks while you worked in high school during summers. There are, however, ways to mitigate stress!

You could handle up to 3 communication lines daily with Airbnb: some inquiries from interested guests.

- Important information for guests arriving soon.

- Issues and requests from guests staying at home at the moment
- You don't feel like the number of messages you're receiving is daunting most days. But some days, it just seems as if the words come in from all directions. You can have a co-host or a management service, and many of the famous names and questions can be automated. You'll know how to get rid of the bad comments when you start learning, and how to have proper Airbnb host etiquette. Your House Rules are going to be ironclad, and you are going to win all your disagreements over the Resolution Centre.
- **A Logistical Challenge**

When we talk about filling the calendar for a short-term rental, there's a lot more work compared with long-term rentals. You will need to be marketing regularly and to make sure that your rates are current and affordable. To avoid double bookings, you would need to be vigilant in syncing calendars across various booking channels. Coordination with multiple vendors, in particular cleaning service, will be required. You would also need to ensure you have all the relevant approvals you need in place.

- **Short term Hotel Taxes and Occupancy Taxes**

A lot of jurisdictions will see the Airbnb business as close to a hotel business. It is considered one of the cons of Airbnb. Therefore, they're likely going to want action terminated. For most countries, it is not unusual to have a temporary rental tax or a short-term occupancy tax of more than 10%. Usually, a month's stay or longer is not subject to these taxes; however, if you allow someone to stay in your Airbnb listing for so long, they can gain tenant rights and refuse to leave!

- **You Likely Have Less Freedom to Travel**

Do you love traveling? We are doing so, too! Yet you can't just go out of town whenever you want, as Airbnb hosts.

You either have to make sure that the dates for your trip are set well in advance, or make sure you have a co-host ready to take care of your place while you're gone. We can say, Airbnb needs you to be more hands-on than the typical landlord you would need to be. You will lead your own separate life as a landlord, and earn your monthly rent once a month. Not so for Airbnb. It has many advantages, but you'll need to be willing to lose a measure of freedom in your daily life to enjoy them.

- **There is Less Early Profit**

You can rent out your house as an entirely different person as a landlord, with the exception generally of the major appliances. Your home has to be furnished entirely: from furniture to beds, towels, and sheets, to toiletries and probably even supplies for the kitchen. And with the competitive scenery of Airbnb, you can't just pick up some collection of old, unattractive objects. Airbnb got its big cut by making a conscious choice to focus heavily on beautiful photo-filled homes. Will you break the bank to get a beautiful house that looks appealing on pictures? No. No. But you'll probably need to spend more money upfront than you would if you'd just rent your room to long-term tenants. Now, your upfront cost will be much lower if you only intend to rent a place in your personal Airbnb residence instead of a completely separate house. But the purpose of this subject to find the best use of an investment property, so it doesn't relate to this topic to rent out a room in your home.

## 8.3 Benefits to Real Estate Agents on Airbnb

Most real estate agents are receiving relatively new inquiries these days: discovering properties that can be turned into short-term rentals from Airbnb.

As we all know it well that it was founded in 2008, Airbnb is a privately owned website that allows homeowners to rent out their room to visitors who are looking for a temporary place to stay, most likely for vacation or business trips. To the uninformed, the best way to describe it is: it is a Craigslist for renting space every night. Unlike the business model of hotels/motels, the proprietor can rent the property directly. Property owners around the world turn their areas into vitally critical financial assets. And the deal is particularly lucrative in places where space, such as holiday spots and other tourist destinations, is limited or costly. It is free and user-friendly to list a property on Airbnb, enabling hosts to upload photos, set rental conditions, write descriptions, and specify hosting dates.

The company makes money by paying both visitors (6-12% of total rental fees) and hosts (around 3% of overall Airbnb site earnings). Now a financial powerhouse and a scraper of the mainstream $550 billion global hospitality industry is what began out as a trickle. The business was estimated at $31 billion as of May 2017. It lists one and a half million properties in 190 countries. The company started as a marketplace for temporary accommodation in rooms (even couches). Still, a growing trend is to market whole properties, some of which are available for a particular Airbnb purpose year-round. Potential Airbnb properties are getting the attention of both amateur and professional investors. Real estate agents who are looking for increased commissions and property owners who are looking for revenue streams can team up to win.

A New York Attorney General's 2014 report found that 94 percent of New York City's Airbnb hosts rented out two units or less. The other 6 percent of hosts reported between 3 groups and 272.

The hosts won a $168 million aggregate and were responsible for over one-third of all city reservations and revenues. Airbnb appeals to business and leisure travelers alike. About 25 percent of leisure travelers are expected to book a stay at Airbnb at least once, up from 19 percent in 2016, according to Morgan Stanley Research. The study also estimated that as of 2017, 23 percent of business travelers would be using Airbnb, up from 18 percent the year before. Half of those who made use of Airbnb in 2016 replaced a conventional hotel stay.

It shows enormous potential for real estate agents, who can warn customers that properties purchased for rent will possibly cover a full monthly mortgage payment. Airbnb has been an immediate hit with Millennials because they are all about renting, not buying. They could, however, be convinced that buying a property for temporary rent could be a lucrative startup business. Airbnb could also be a good option for consumers who can't sell their property immediately. You may consider suggesting that they will turn it to an Airbnb destination until a buyer arrives. Another idea for potential buyers: try the area before you purchase, suggesting the owners use Airbnb as a trial period to encourage the potential buyers to live in the property for a limited time.

This program is not appropriate for everyone. Note Airbnb does not allow the automatic transfer of listings to new owners. Your client should also understand any tax requirements which involve rentals from Airbnb.

Another consideration: Is the property in a seasonal setting? Can this be rented successfully year-round? Additionally, if a property has already been tried as an Airbnb rental and has not received many rentals. Then there may be an underlying (or visible) explanation for this. Remember that both positive and negative comments about a property are recorded by renters, who are often researched by potential renters. Any complaints could stick and discourage future tenants.

# Conclusion

Airbnb rental investment is a way of earning money by sharing a spared room or a whole apartment. Airbnb is the right choice because short term rentals are getting their place in the market and are giving higher income. How you can earn from Airbnb rentals without owning property or investment is a big question in minds. But yes, it possible. There are many ways to make bucks from Airbnb without any capital, and even one can earn in six-figures within a short time working smartly. You can be a property manager on Airbnb and can make a deal with the landlord about the re-renting of the house after knowing the legislation in your region. Being a property manager, you can serve your guests by looking at their check-ins and check-outs or maybe by getting information from the guests. You can also get bucks by sharing your experiences with the visitors if you got some talent. You can give a cooking class or guide them about the city's history. You can guide them in hiking the mountains and provide them with a bike ride through your city. You can use Airbnb rental arbitrage for earning money passively. For doing this, you need to start with a business plan, make the team, a co-host, a marketing search, properties to find, the listing of properties, and proper pricing. As most guests prefer Airbnb for its lesser prices than hotels, therefore, reasonable pricing must be your consideration. These things will lead you to success within minimum time.

If you are hosting, then listing is the most crucial factor to present your availabilities. Showing the accommodation with good photos can be a road to your success as these photographs will attract the tenants to book the apartment.

So, for staying top in the rankings on Airbnb, a host needs some peculiar characteristics as he is the main person responsible for managing the place by keeping it in optimum condition.

You can keep the apartment clean with the help of the relevant team and make sure of the availability of accessories. You can meet the guest's demand more accurately by checking their reviews from time to time. Getting positive reviews will give you more availability of tenants. When you are entering a field, you must know its advantages and disadvantages. Airbnb is going to provide you with many benefits, along with money. You will be a better communicator, more knowledge, and experience by working with excellent hospitality. But yes, it may be a slow process if you already have not any particular skill or it will need your full-time availability to attend the guests. So, I can conclude this all by saying that Airbnb vacation rentals are going to give you the profit you have never imagined if you put your head down and work diligently on this!

# References

Bnb Duck. (2020). *9 ways to make money on Airbnb without owning property - Bnb Duck.* [online] Available at: **https://bnbduck.com/9-ways-to-make-money-on-airbnb-without-owning-property/**.

Get Paid For Your Pad. (2020). *How to Start Airbnb Arbitrage and What to Look Out For.* [online] Available at: **https://getpaidforyourpad.com/blog/rental-arbitrage/**.

Airbnb Handsfree. (2020). *Common Characteristics of Airbnb's Most Successful Rentals – Airbnb Handsfree.* [online] Available at: **https://airbnbhandsfree.com.au/our-blog/common-characteristics-airbnbs-successful-rentals/**.

Team, G. (2020). *A Step-by-Step Guide on How to List on Airbnb - Guesty.* [online] Guesty. Available at: **https://www.guesty.com/blog/step-by-step-guide-how-to-list-on-airbnb/**.

FortuneBuilders. (2020). *Airbnb Rental Strategy For The Savvy Investor | FortuneBuilders.* [online] Available at: **https://www.fortunebuilders.com/airbnb-rentals/**.

The Wallet Wise Guy. (2020). *The 3 Biggest Pros and Cons of Airbnb Hosting..* [online] Available at: **https://walletwiseguy.com/the-pros-and-cons-of-airbnb-for-investment-property/**.

Great Dwellings. (2020). *Benefits of Becoming an Airbnb Host.* [online] Available at: **https://greatdwellings.com/benefits-becoming-airbnb-host/**.

Airbnb », G. and Rentals, P. (2020). *Pros and Cons of Airbnb & Short Term Rentals - AirHost Academy.* [online] AirHost Academy. Available at: **https://airhostacademy.com/pros-and-cons-of-airbnb/**.

www.ingramcontent.com/pod-product-compliance
Lightning Source LLC
Chambersburg PA
CBHW021439210526
45463CB00002B/578